Quality in the Early

Quality in the Early Years

Edited by Emma Slaughter

 Open University Press

Open University Press
McGraw-Hill Education
8th Floor
338 Euston Road
London
NW1 3BH

email: enquiries@openup.co.uk
world wide web: www.openup.co.uk

and Two Penn Plaza, New York, NY 10121-2289, USA

First published 2016

Copyright © Emma Slaughter, 2016

All rights reserved. Except for the quotation of short passages for the purposes
of criticism and review, no part of this publication may be reproduced, stored
in a retrieval system, or transmitted, in any form or by any means, electronic,
mechanical, photocopying, recording or otherwise, without the prior written
permission of the publisher or a licence from the Copyright Licensing Agency
Limited. Details of such licences (for reprographic reproduction) may be obtained
from the Copyright Licensing Agency Ltd of Saffron House, 6–10 Kirby Street,
London EC1N 8TS.

A catalogue record of this book is available from the British Library

ISBN-13: 978-0-33-526222-9
ISBN-10: 0-33-526222-8
eISBN: 978-0-33-526223-6

Library of Congress Cataloging-in-Publication Data
CIP data applied for

Typeset by SPi Global

Printed and bound by CPI Group (UK) Ltd, Croydon, CRO 4YY

Fictitious names of companies, products, people, characters and/or
data that may be used herein (in case studies or in examples) are not
intended to represent any real individual, company, product or event.

J Godding

Praise for this book

"Quality in the Early Years, edited by Emma Slaughter, provides important and pertinent discussions to support considerations for those working with young children. It gives different perspectives on the notion of quality from various viewpoints, for example research findings or international contexts. The book is highly relevant for practitioners, professionals and students who are concerned about identifying issues surrounding the meaning of quality, with helpful reflections for the reader of their early years provision, pedagogy and practice."

Dr Pat Beckley, Bishop Grosseteste University, UK

Contents

List of contributors viii

List of abbreviations and acronyms x

Introduction xii

1: **Quality Care and Education in the Early Years** 1
Emma Slaughter and Patrick Carmichael

2: **Quality Experiences for Babies and Very Young Children** 16
Sarah Cousins and Perry Knight

3: **Quality Early Years Environments** 30
Abigail Gosling

4: **Developing Quality Relationships** 50
Julie Beams

5: **Quality in the Early Years Curriculum** 73
Perry Knight

6: **Policies for Quality Early Years Provision** 89
Sarah Cousins

7: **Quality Education and Care for Vulnerable Children** 100
Isabelle Brodie

8: **Quality Early Years Professionals** 118
Emma Slaughter

9: **International Perspectives on Quality in Early Years Education** 138
Patrick Carmichael

10: **Quality in Early Years Research** 152
Patrick Carmichael

Index 164

Contributors

Julie Beams

Julie Beams is a senior lecturer in Early Years Education at the University of Bedfordshire, and has co-ordinated and taught on EYRS, undergraduate and foundation degree programmes of study. Prior to this, she worked as a local authority advisory teacher and a children's centre teacher and has held a number of teaching and leadership roles in primary schools and day nursery provision. Julie's professional interests include leadership and the development of professionalism and also the rights, well-being and learning needs of young children, particularly the under-twos as schools extend their provision to include this age group.

Isabelle Brodie

Isabelle Brodie is a teacher and researcher at the University of Bedfordshire. She has worked as a researcher for some 20 years in areas relating to child welfare, with a particular interest in the education of children in care. She has also worked for the National Evaluation of Sure Start at Birkbeck College and the NCB. More recently she has also worked on a number of research studies relating to child sexual exploitation, including work for the NSPCC, the Scottish Government and the Office of the Children's Commissioner in England.

Patrick Carmichael

Patrick Carmichael is Professor of Education at the University of Bedfordshire. Formerly a teacher, he has conducted research and written widely on areas of education including the design of learning technologies, research methods, research ethics, and interdisciplinary and inter-professional working.

Sarah Cousins

Sarah Cousins was formerly an early years teacher and phase leader in schools, early years consultant for local authority, course leader for early years degrees and portfolio leader for undergraduate and postgraduate education courses. Sarah is now the director of early years programmes at the Centre for Lifelong Learning at the University of Warwick and an Early Years Ofsted inspector. Her research interests are on the importance of establishing loving relationships with children in education and care settings, emotional learning and professionalism. Sarah is also very interested in appropriate research methodologies for research about affective aspects of work with very young children.

Abigail Gosling

Abigail Gosling is currently the course co-ordinator for the BA(Hons) Early Years Education degree at the University of Bedfordshire. Abigail began her teaching career in the secondary phase in schools in Manchester and Bedford teaching A-level and GCSE English. She then retrained at the Froebel Institute and subsequently taught extensively throughout the early years phase, in both PVI settings and maintained nursery schools and primary schools. She has worked for two local authorities as an adviser for early years education supporting a variety of settings, maintained, private and voluntary settings, and children's centres to improve the learning and teaching for young children, and with the QCDA on the EYFS Registered Moderator Accreditation programme.

Perry Knight

Perry Knight leads early years within the Department of Teacher Education at the University of Bedfordshire . Perry has worked in education as a middle and senior leader for 20 years and has taught across contexts in secondary, all-through and special education. To date, he has been part of a senior leadership team within an all-age academy, and more recently a 7–19 residential school for young people with a primary diagnosis of autism. In addition, Perry has provided consultancy for primary schools transitioning into new academies, early years, and strategies for working with children with ASD. Perry's PhD, awarded from the University of Bath in 2014, considered the contexts of children's transition from primary to secondary. More recently, his research focuses on learning transitions from birth to primary school and environmental therapies to support young children and their learning.

Emma Slaughter

Emma Slaughter has a career which originated in leading children's centres and early years services in Local Authorities. This is coupled with academic teaching roles in Higher Education Institutions and extensive consultancy experience within children's services nationally. She has a particular interest in informal learning within multi-agency contexts, and this has been the focus of her research at Masters and Doctoral level.

Abbreviations and Acronyms

ASD	Autistic Spectrum Disorders
BERA	British Educational Research Association
BSA	British Sociological Association
CAF	Common Assessment Framework
CIS	Caregiver Interaction Scale
CPD	Continuing Professional Development
CRC	Convention on the Rights of the Child
CWDC	Children's Workforce Development Council
DCSF	Department for Children, Schools and Families (precursor of DFE, 2007–2010)
DfE	Department for Education
DfES	Department for Education and Skills (precursor of DFE, 2001–2007)
ECaT	Every Child a Talker
ECEC	Early Childhood Education and Care
ECERS	Early Childhood Environment Rating Scale
ECERS-E	Early Childhood Environment Rating Scale Extension
ECERS-R	Early Childhood Environment Rating Scale (Revised)
EEF	Education Endowment Foundation
EPPE	Effective Provision of Pre-School Education (Project)
ERS	Environment Rating Scales
EU	European Union
EYFS	Early Years Foundation Stage
EYFSP	Early Years Foundation Stage Profile
EYITT	Early Years Initial Teacher Training
EYPS	Early Years Professional Status
EYTS	Early Years Teacher Status
EYTSEN	Early Years Transition and Special Educational Needs (Project)
FCCERS	Family Child Care Environment Rating Scale
ICT	Information and Communications Technology
ITERS-R	The Infant and Toddler Environment Rating Scale (Revised)
NCB	National Children's Bureau
NDNA	National Day Nurseries Association
NICHD	National Institute of Child Health and Human Development
NQIN	National Quality Improvement Network
NSPCC	National Society for the Prevention of Cruelty to Children
OECD	Organization for Economic Co-operation and Development
Ofsted	Office for Standards in Education, Children's Services and Skills

ORCE	Observational Record of the Caregiving Environment
QCDA	Qualifications and Curriculum Development Agency
QTS	Qualified Teacher Status
REPEY	Researching Effective Pedagogy in the Early Years (Project)
SACERS	School-Age Care Environment Rating Scale
SSLP	Sure Start Local Programmes
SEN	Special Educational Needs
SEND	Special Educational Needs and Disabilities
UNESCO	United Nations Economic, Scientific and Cultural Organization
UNICEF	United Nations (Emergency) Children's Fund

Introduction

Emma Slaughter

Whether you are about to embark on undergraduate study, or are already working in the field of early years, this book is written with you in mind. Its purpose is to provoke and challenge your own personal reflections on some of the key aspects of early years practice in order that you will come to develop and understand your own idea of what 'quality' early years provision means.

Naturally, as an early years professional, you have an interest in delivering high-quality provision for very young children and you understand why this is so important in the lives of children – both in the immediate and longer-term sense. This book seeks to engage you in your own personal reflections with a view to constructing your own definition or understanding of what you consider quality early years provision to be – the attributes, characteristics, skills and principles that form the vital ingredients of ensuring 'quality'.

We start in Chapter 1 by recognizing that 'quality in early years' is a term frequently and justifiably referred to within the field, yet it is often used without clarification or definition. The aim of this book is to take you on a journey of constructing and reconstructing your own thoughts, ideas and beliefs about what is important in order to achieve 'quality' in your own pedagogical practice and, more importantly, understanding 'why' you hold such views of beliefs.

Individual chapters explore and provide an insight into a range of key aspects of early years practice. Some chapters focus on the very practical aspects of day-to-day practice (what leads to a quality environment, how might quality differ when working with babies or vulnerable children, and so on) and some consider the more procedural-based aspects of pedagogical practice (ensuring quality policies and how quality might be represented within curriculums, and so on). Towards the end of the book you are invited to consider your own idea of quality alongside expectations of quality in international early years contexts, examining more closely the social and cultural influences at play. Once you have identified your own notion of what quality provision looks like and also your rationale for why you believe this, you will then conclude your journey through this book by using it as a foundation for how you might undertake quality research and enquiry with very young children – whether that is in your existing setting, or as you move into a new setting, or as you prepare to undertake research for the purpose of a dissertation.

Written by experts within their individual fields, the chapters may be read in a linear fashion, so starting at Chapter 1 and moving through individual chapters consecutively until you reach the end, or you may prefer to use it as a handbook or resource for you to move through at your own pace and order depending on your specific area of interest at any one time. However, it is recommended that you start with Chapter 1 first as subsequent chapters will relate back to some of the initial reflections encouraged here, especially in relation to your own early ideas of what the most important characteristics of early years provision are.

Each chapter includes a series of 'reflection points', which are designed to deepen your understanding and engage you in personal reflection about the topic of the chapter. Reflection Points may take the form of inviting you to consider how this new knowledge might be applied in practice, or what the implications might be. Similarly, they may ask you to discuss your thoughts with others to share ideas and perspectives. These reflection points, therefore, form a vital part of the learning within each chapter and the book as a whole. Many of the reflection points relate to one another, so you will find it helpful to retain your reflective notes even after you have completed a chapter. Furthermore, you may wish to reflect on questions posed at a later date to see how your ideas change as your learning and understanding develops.

Within each chapter, the authors present their own ideas alongside other published works in order to arouse challenge in individual thinking. As such, you may notice that your reflections and ideas change and adjust as you move through the publication – this is good as it means you are building, accommodating and assimilating these into new thoughts and understanding.

Enjoy the journey!

1 Quality care and education in the early years

Emma Slaughter and Patrick Carmichael

Educational policy documents frequently talk about 'high-quality provision' and 'high-quality practice' and these are phrases that anyone working in education will hear on a frequent basis in both formal and informal discussions; not least, in early years settings. But all too often, these terms are used without any real clarity and are not defined, questioned or even open to critique. Instead, there is often an assumption that these are 'givens' about which everyone agrees. After all, who could possibly not think 'quality education' or 'quality care' are good ideas?

Starting points: the Early Years Foundation Stage (EYFS) and the National Quality Improvement Network (NQIN)

Introduced in 2008, the EYFS statutory framework was the first statutory (rather than simply advisory) curriculum for children under 5 years old in England. Essentially a play-based curriculum, drawing from the previous *Birth to Three Matters* framework (Department for Education and Skills, 2002) and *Curriculum Guidance for the Foundation Stage* (Department for Education and Employment, 2000), the EYFS outlined expected norms of development for children from birth through to the end of their year in reception and expectations of providers. Following the Tickell Review in 2011 (Department for Education and Employment, 2000), the EYFS underwent significant revisions in 2012 (Department for Education, 2012b), and then more minor revisions in 2014 (Department for Education, 2014a).

A reading of the EYFS statutory framework tends to encourage the idea that quality is non-negotiable: it is described as 'giving all professionals a set of common principles and commitments to deliver quality early education and childcare experiences to all children' (The Children's Partnership, undated), on the basis that it is a combination of good parenting and quality early learning that give children the best life chances (Department for Education, 2014a, p. 5). As well as talking in general terms about quality provision and care, it goes on to identify the importance of quality learning experiences and a quality workforce (Department for Education, 2014a, p. 10), quality settings (2014a, p. 16) and defines the role of the Office for Standards in Education, Children's Service and Skills (Ofsted) in quality assurance (2014a, p. 4). As this framework is statutory, it forms the basis of much of the training, planning, practice and evaluation of early years provision. But while it talks throughout about 'quality' and helpfully suggests that this involves the elements mentioned above, it provides little detail on why these are so important, how quality is defined and recognized, and how quality practice can be developed and sustained.

At the same time, we can infer how quality is to be understood by looking at the purposes ascribed to early years education, and the inspection regime that is implemented by Ofsted. The 2012 revision of the EYFS statutory framework introduced the notion of 'school readiness', suggesting that high-quality early years practice is that which enables children to be 'ready for school'. In England, although children must be in education following the term after their fifth birthday, the trend is for children to be 'in school' and have experiences governed by statutory frameworks from an increasingly early age (Department for Education, 2014b). This is in contrast to many other countries (including those, like Finland and Sweden, whose education systems are seen as being very effective) where children are not expected to begin formal schooling until a later age.

Early years providers (whether they are childminders, schools, nurseries, preschools or Children's Centres) are not only governed by the EYFS statutory framework but are inspected by Ofsted. As a non-ministerial government department, Ofsted inspects and regulates services that care for children and young people, as well as services providing education and skills for learners of all ages. With the aim of improving standards and attainment by children, it inspects the 'quality' of provision against a predetermined inspection framework which outlines grade descriptors that determine thresholds for defining practice as 'inadequate', 'requiring improvement', 'good' or 'outstanding'. Emphasis is placed on educational data, with a strong message that high-quality early years practice results in higher educational attainment of young children against the prescribed developmental norms set out in the EYFS statutory framework.

There are other perspectives on quality, however. The National Children's Bureau (NCB) National Quality Improvement Network (NQIN) was set up in 2000 to provide quality assurance of early years settings. However, it approached this in a different way to the EYFS and it is clear in its definition of quality that emerges through reflection, consultation and engagement with parents, and identifies its principal aim as being to inspire a community of practitioners who are confident in their use of self-evaluation, for improved outcomes of children, and to narrow the gap (National Children's Bureau, 2013). The NQIN website is, accordingly, a rich source of case studies and evaluations that reflect its commitments to participation and consultation. The question this raises, of course, is how other early years providers can apply these examples, without falling into the trap of trying to replicate a generic 'best practice' regardless of its own situations and the settings in which it works.

Already, we have two slightly different perspectives on quality. One, the EYFS, speaks primarily about aspects of **service provision** underpinned by

common principles and reinforced by a **quality assurance regime** implemented by Ofsted; the other, the NQIN, although also concerned with quality assurance, stresses the importance of early years practitioners **consulting parents** and **evaluating their own practice**. And there are more to come! But the approach we will take in this book is not to argue for one of these perspectives over any other. Instead, as we explained in the Introductory chapter, we will invite you to develop your own understandings of 'quality' in relation to your own practice, the settings in which you work and those with whom you work. It is through processes of reflection both on your own notion of quality and those encapsulated in documents like the EYFS and the NQIN 'principles' that you will develop your own quality practice. So this is a good point to introduce the first of the 'reflection points' that will guide you through the remainder of the book.

Reflection point 1.1

Your first two questions:

- What do you think are the most important aspects of 'good quality practice' in early years provision? *These might come from your experience as a child; through observations of children with whom you have worked; as a parent or carer; or it might come from learning about child development.*
- Do you think there are any aspects of quality, which are 'non-negotiable', while others need to be developed through consultation? If the latter, who should be involved in that consultation?

You might do this as a list, or a 'mind-map', or in some other format, but you will need to return to these initial thoughts at later points in the book, so be prepared to see that what you write now changes as your experience and understandings develop.

Other perspectives on quality in the early years

While the EYFS statutory framework may have a great influence on much of the day-to-day practice in early years settings, there are other frameworks and ideas of quality that also exist—sometimes coexisting, and sometimes challenging or providing implicit or explicit critique of any normative notions. Some of these seek to provide evaluation frameworks, expressed as checklists of features and indicators of quality. In general, these standardized tests and scales are supplemented by more detailed interviews of staff and observational methods in order to inform judgements because 'quality' is 'both objective in terms of characteristics and subjective in terms of views' (Siraj-Blatchford & Wong, 1999, p. 14); or they are 'mapped' to broader frameworks such as those used by Ofsted (Mathers, Singler, & Karemaker, 2012, pp. 65–67).

Measures of interaction quality

There are a number of widely used observational tools that are used to measure the quality of specific aspects of early years environments. These tend to focus on observable measures of interaction and while limited in scope, they are popular because they are relatively easy to use and reliable; that is, by reducing the need for subjective judgements, they allow information to be collected consistently by different observers. Because they concentrate on interactions between carers and children, and are not reliant upon a specific social context or physical environment, they can be used in any setting, allowing comparisons across, for example, a child's home, a carer's home, a centre or a school.

The Arnett Caregiver Interaction Scale (CIS) (Arnett, 1989) uses an inventory of 26 actions and maps these to four dimensions: 'sensitivity', 'harshness', 'detachment' and 'permissiveness'. The items in the inventory and their analysis, which is based on a view of parenting 'styles', articulate particular views both of early learning and quality care, some of which are open to question. Despite this, the CIS has been widely used, particularly in the USA, although it has recently been criticised both on the grounds of the validity of the dimensions and the notions of quality care on which it is based (Colwell, Gordon, Fujimoto, Kaestner, & Korenman, 2013). The Observational Record of the Caregiving Environment (ORCE), published in 1996 by the US National Institute of Child Health and Human Development (NICHD Early Child Care Research Network, 2002) is also widely used tool, and, again, focuses on the frequency and quality of behaviours toward children.

Environment Rating Scales (ERS)

Other observational instruments are broader in their scope than those which focus on the carer, and the most widely used of these are the ERS initially developed at the University of North Carolina and used in a wide range of settings around the world. The ERS family includes:

- The Early Childhood Environment Rating Scale (Revised) (ECERS-R), designed to assess provision for children from 30 months to 5 years old (Harms, Clifford, & Cryer, 2005).
- The Infant and Toddler Environment Rating Scale (Revised) (ITERS-R), designed to assess provision for children from birth to 30 months old (Harms, Cryer, & Clifford, 2006).
- The Early Childhood Environment Rating Scale Extension (ECERS-E), designed to assess curricular provision in literacy, mathematics and science for children aged 3– to 5 years old in more detail than the ECERS-R scale (Sylva, Siraj-Blatchford, & Taggart, 2010).

There are also two additional scales for assessing the quality of home-based provision: the Family Childcare Environment Rating Scale (FCCERS) for children from birth to 12 years old) (Harms, Cryer, & Clifford, 2007) and the School-Age Care Environment Rating Scale (SACERS) designed to assess out-of-school provision for children of school age (Harms, Jacobs, & White, 2013).

Each of these scales comprises a range of statements or 'indicators' that can evaluate the quality of the early years environment. These indicators are cumulative, and aim to provide a rigorous and consistent means of measuring quality—and, therefore, improvement in quality—over time. The ECERS-R and ITERS-R scales evaluate aspects of quality on 7-point scales from 1 (inadequate) to 7 (excellent):

- *Space and furnishings*: for example, room layout, accessibility of resources, display.
- *Personal care routines*: for example, attention to welfare requirements, health and safety and provision for sleeping.
- *Language and reasoning*: supporting children's communication, language and literacy development and critical thinking.
- *Activities*: provision of an exciting and accessible learning environment and the availability of resources to support specific types of play.
- *Interaction*: patterns of supervision and support for social interactions.
- *Programme structure*: opportunities for children to access their own curriculum, and the planning schedules of routines to meet children's needs.
- *Provision for parents and staff*: for example, partnership with parents and opportunities for staff training and development.

The full lists are summarized very clearly in a report by Mathers et al. (2012, pp. 103–110) where they state that the idea of what constitutes an early years 'environment' is defined broadly, and assessing quality does not focus on interactions, like ORCE or CIS. Using these scales to their full extent also involves looking beyond the physical surroundings, or the curriculum, or the specific activities in which children are involved to think about staffing, training and relationships: this is a pattern that is developed in the studies we now turn to, and which we will explore further in this book as a whole.

SPEEL: Study of pedagogical effectiveness in early learning

The SPEEL project, despite its focus on pedagogy, set out to consider quality in 'inclusionary' terms rather than through input and output measures (Moyles, Adams, & Musgrove, 2002, p. 13). SPEEL aimed to identify the embedded characteristics of effective pedagogy in the early years and was conducted primarily through engagement with those involved in delivery of early years education with 3–5-year-olds. As well as identifying the knowledge, understanding and skills that practitioners needed to hold in order to be 'effective' in their pedagogical practice, it also highlighted the importance of parental partnerships, leadership and management, as well as the role of record keeping and documentation.

Effective Provision of Pre-School Education (EPPE)

The EPPE project was a major longitudinal study of young children's educational experiences and development between 3 and 7 years old (Sylva, Melhuish, Sammons, Siraj-Blatchford, & Taggart, 2004). What the EPPE project defined was not only the characteristics of 'quality' practice in both 'structure' and 'processes' (Sylva et al., 2004, p. 5), but also what impact these had on children's longer-term outcomes, and the project's research demonstrated the positive effects of high-quality provision on children's intellectual, social and behavioural development measured at primary school entry as well as at the end of Key Stage 1 (that is, at 7 years old). The impact was particularly marked for children who experienced disadvantages, especially where they accessed preschool provision alongside children from a mixture of social backgrounds.

The project used the ECERS-R and ECERS-E scales to characterize the various settings in which the project worked and the CIS scale was used to assess the patterns of interactions between children and carers in these settings and more widely (Sylva et al., 2004, pp. 6–7). Critically, however, these scales were used alongside other, qualitative methods, allowing case studies of centres to be developed and broader understandings of 'effectiveness' and 'quality' to emerge. While many of these quality indicators were easily defined (for example, the level of qualifications of staff, particularly managers, and the periods of time spent by children in settings), others included the relative importance attached to social and educational development, with the most effective settings being those that saw these as being complementary and equal in importance (Sylva et al., 2004, p. 71). The EPPE project recognized that the quality of provision or practice cannot be reduced to its 'effectiveness', which is described as 'a necessary but insufficient component of quality on its own' (Sylva et al., 2004, pp. 6–7). As a longitudinal study, however, effectiveness and quality is ultimately measured on the grounds of subsequent educational attainment—at the end of the EYFS or at the end of Key Stage 1. So now we have an idea of quality which is in some ways broader than one that is defined in terms of observable features or behaviours (like CIS or ORCE), but at the same time demands that we take into account the measurable outcomes and impacts of those features and behaviours. This, of course, raises another question; namely, which outcomes and impacts we should consider as the longer-term indicators of quality provision.

Researching Effective Pedagogy in the Early Years (REPEY)

The large-scale and longitudinal design of the EPPE project has led to a series of related research activities, analyses and reports. In one of these, the REPEY, the *pedagogical* practice in 12 of the most effective EPPE settings were studied in detail. The project highlighted a number of key aspects of practice:

- Support for child-initiated verbal interactions and dialogues to encourage 'sustained shared thinking'.

- Sharing of child-related information between parents and staff with parents involved in decision making about their child's learning.

- Support for parents in developing the home education environment to support children's learning.

- Discipline and behaviour policies that prioritize rationalizing and talking through conflicts. (Siraj-Blatchford, Sylva, Muttock, Gilden, & Bell, 2002, pp. 10–12)

The Early Years Transitions and Special Educational Needs (EYTSEN)

In a further extension of the EYTSEN project, (Sammons et al. 2003) explored provision for children considered to be 'at risk' of their cognitive, or social and behavioural development. For those 'at risk' as a result of poor cognitive development, integrated centres and nursery schools were seen to be particularly beneficial, and for those 'at risk' in terms of poor social behaviour, it was rather integrated centres, nursery classes and playgroups that were particularly beneficial.

Just as in the EPPE studies as a whole, it was those children with little or no experience of attending any preschool setting (and whose care was solely based in the home) that were judged to be significantly 'at risk' for all measures of cognitive development at entry to primary school and more were also at heightened risk of having poor social skills. For these often multiple disadvantaged children, the importance of appropriate, high-quality care and education was of even greater significance, and the EYTSEN project highlighted the correlation between high-quality care (measured in terms of CIS and ECERS scales, and through qualitative methods) and the progress on cognitive measures made by children by the time they entered primary school. That said, provision varied widely, and the case for early years education as a means of overcoming social and behavioural problems was less marked (Sammons et al., 2003, p. 19).

The Wolverhampton early years professional framework study

The theme of leadership of early years practice that featured in the EPPE and related studies was also identified in a subsequent evaluation of the impact of the introduction of Early Years Professional Status (EYPS) across different settings. EYPS was launched in 2007 to provide a standard for the 'professional skills, knowledge and practice experience to be required of someone taking a coordinating role' in early years settings (Department for Education and Skills, 2006, p. 30). The Children's Workforce Development Council (CWDC) commissioned the study in 2009 and the report was published after the change in government in 2010. In this report, the authors discuss the evolution of the notions of professionalism and leadership in early years and their relationship to quality provision (Hadfield et al., 2012). While the report does not offer a conclusive judgement as to whether 'professional status' itself impacted on quality outcomes, it draws on ideas of 'pedagogical leadership' and highlights the importance of 'practice leadership' as involving 'a combination of modelling, mentoring and formal professional development . . . [that has become] embedded in the settings' culture' (Hadfield et al., 2012, p. 7). We will return to discuss leadership in more detail in later chapters.

Reflection point 1.2

If you have spent time in an early years setting, think back to the way in which the staff there worked with you.

- The 'Wolverhampton' EYPS evaluation describes 'practice leadership' as involving a combination of modelling, mentoring and formal professional development, embedded in the settings' culture. What roles did the early years practitioners with whom you worked play in contributing to quality provision? How did they help you learn?
- In larger, more complex settings such as schools or Children's Centres, how can leadership of practice and therefore quality provision be effectively monitored, developed and sustained? Does all leadership need to be 'formal' with a specific assigned person in role, or do you agree with the Wolverhampton Evaluation when it says that other staff should be involved in 'informal' and 'ollective' approaches to leading practice? (Hadfield et al., 2012, p. 7)

We will return to these questions and meet the idea of 'leaderful practice' in later chapters, but for now try and keep in mind this idea of quality provision as being an aspect of practice leadership, and this practice not being confined to those at the top of the organizational chart in the early years setting

---

Stakeholders, quality and early years practice

As we look at these various approaches to defining, supporting and developing quality care, education and practice, it is evident that they have been developed by different individuals, groups and agencies, each with their own concerns and 'lenses' on quality. These reflect differences in thinking about the purposes of early years education and care, as well as ideas about the role, status and training of the practitioners involved in their provision. This is the case in any educational system, where the interests of government, educators, parents, employers and, of course, learners themselves, may diverge widely. But the inherently multi-agency nature of early years settings, provision and practice; the wide range of disciplinary backgrounds of the practitioners involved and the centrality of early years issues in family and community life, highlights these differences.

Even when all these different agencies and individuals agree that the 'child is at the centre' of early years education and care, and that quality should ultimately reflect their interests, they may have different ideas about what that means in practice. In the review document by Mathers et al. (2012), the authors discuss the views of three key stakeholder groups: parents and carers, providers (teachers and managers) and local authority staff. Focus groups from across these groups agreed that quality early years practice was grounded in 'warm and nurturing relationships' and provided well-planned activities that promoted learning, development and peer-to-peer interactions. While the environment was seen as an important contributor to this, it was no substitute for well-trained and caring staff, and a 'key person' approach in which one person was responsible for each child and provided a first point of contact for parents and carers was well-regarded (Mathers et al., 2012, p. 33).

There were, however, some notable differences: providers and local authority staff saw the qualifications and experience of staff, and specifically a good knowledge of children development as important, while parents placed more emphasis on a stable staff who were warm, friendly and approachable. But perhaps the most interesting difference was that while providers and local authority participants saw early years provision involving both education and care (echoing findings of the EPPE project and other research), parents reported that while it was important that settings helped to ensure their children made progress, they did not view early years as being primarily about 'education', which they associated with formal schooling (Mathers et al., 2012, p. 34).

There are, of course, other stakeholders with interests in early years provision and practice, ranging from health workers, social workers to providers of other public services from housing and transport, to libraries and parks. Each of these might look at the same child, or family, or early years setting, in different ways, using different conceptual frameworks and language. This is made even more challenging when each of the stakeholders is driven by different sets of outcome measures or targets. While they may all be concerned with locating the child at the centre of their provision, they may all see them as a 'case' of something different: social workers may see them as being 'at risk' because of family circumstances while for health workers they may be a priority because they have a poor diet and are failing to put on weight. At the same time, in the nursery, their teachers may see them through the lens of the EYFS as a child who is not developing 'as expected' and who may fail to achieve the outcomes that comprise a 'good level of development' by the end of the foundation stage. Others may see the child as a potential 'service user': so the local library service may be most concerned that they have had the latest 'bookstart pack', and the organizers of the local charity-funded adventure playground may simply be keen to improve their attendance and see the child as a potential visitor. Add into this a local charity with a remit to support certain priority groups within which the child falls (but who are still keen to demonstrate the impact of their activities), and the situation grows even more complex!

For early years practitioners, especially those 'key persons' responsible for specific children, a major challenge is to support and develop consistent, high-quality practice that takes into account these sometimes contradictory stakeholder perspectives of the children in their care. We will look at these implications of these multiple perspectives in later chapters, particularly Chapter 5 on 'quality relationships'.

A global perspective on quality: UNICEF

An even broader notion of stakeholders and a view of quality education and care as intrinsically connected emerged from the 'rights-based' approach of the United Nations Children's Fund (UNICEF). UNICEF's view of quality is grounded in the *Convention on the Rights of the Child* (UN General Assembly, 1989) and argues for a 'safe, rights-based' and 'child-friendly' education, that is, that goes beyond simply provision and recognises that the child is the primary stakeholder in an education system (United Nations Children's Fund, 2010). This is reflected in the UNICEF view that 'school readiness' involves not just children's readiness for school, but also their families' readiness for school and schools' readiness for children (United Nations Children's Fund, 2011).

In a review of what constitutes quality education, UNICEF presents a model of educational provision and practice, which recognizes the multiple stakeholder perspectives but also argues that quality education depends on far more than simply curriculum design or professional development (United Nations Children's Fund, 2000). UNICEF argues that these count for little if children are malnourished, or simply cannot get to school because of parents' or carers' working patterns, poor transport systems, direct or indirect costs, or threats of violence. Quality educational experiences are characterized by:

- quality of facilities in the educational setting itself, as well as interconnection between these education facilities and other infrastructure. UNICEF highlights the availability of clean water and sanitation, but such concerns are not limited to 'developing country' contexts: many early years settings in the UK are far from ideal in terms of their suitability, location and 'connections' to other services particularly when they are based in buildings not originally designed with early years education in mind

- peaceful, safe environments and the practices that adults use to contribute to children's safety, security and self-confidence

- class size and ratios of adults to children in the setting
- inclusion, both in policy and practice
- close integration with health services: not only are healthy children more likely to attend educational settings, but also the settings they are in can co-ordinate and communicate information, implement health initiatives, and contribute to the education of parents and carers

We will return to discuss some of these issues in more detail in Chapter 9, 'International perspectives on quality in the early years', but for now it is worth keeping in mind that even in 'developed country' contexts with well-established and stable educational systems, it is worth thinking about early years education and care as just one aspect of a complex set of public services, private provision and broader infrastructures that may be changing and where policy decisions and funding priorities in one area may have significant implications for early years practice, provision and outcomes.

More great childcare and EYTS

In this chapter so far, we have considered concepts and measures of quality ranging from those that are focused solely on the interactions between carers and children, to those, like the UNICEF model, which sees early years provision in a much broader context of rights, social and economic frameworks, and multiple stakeholder perspectives. We now turn to the question of how best to prepare early years practitioners to learn about, work in and contribute to quality environments. We have highlighted how various frameworks and research studies have recognized the importance of teachers being involved in professional development, reflecting and sharing practice and seeing themselves as both leaders and learners throughout their careers. If you are currently engaged in an initial teacher training programme, or a programme of training in your own workplace, this will probably be your major concern, and is probably the reason you are reading this book!

So what is the background against which you can develop as an early years practitioner? Clearly, the EYFS provides one set of answers, but it is, as we have seen, couched in terms of the experiences and outcomes for children. But another recent source that sets out how high-quality practice and for that matter the 'high-quality practitioner' are envisaged is the 2013 report *More great childcare: Raising quality and giving parents more choice* (Department for Education, 2013). The UK government commissioned a review of early years training and qualifications, which was published in 2012 and referred to as the 'Nutbrown Report' after its author Cathy Nutbrown (Department for Education, 2012a).

The recommendations that emerged from this report were based on an explicit recognition of the links between quality training and leadership and children's experiences regardless of the setting in which they received education and care, so that:

> Every child is able to experience high quality care and education whatever type of home or group setting they attend; early years staff have a strong professional identity, take pride in their work, and are recognised and valued by parents, other professionals and society as a whole; [and] high quality early education and care is led by well qualified early years practitioners. (Department for Education, 2012a, p. 10).

When the Nutbrown Report was published, there was debate about some of the recommendations it made, most notably about the importance it attached to early years practioners being able to obtain Qualified Teacher Status (QTS), and about the relationship between quality and qualifications (Faux, 2012). The government accepted some of the recommendations of the Nutbrown Report; others were 'accepted in principle' or rejected. *More great childcare* has shaped the environment we see today and defined the kind of training programme on which you may be enrolled. With a bold declaration that 'we know what works in early years education: high quality qualifications and well-trained staff' (Department for Education, 2013, p. 15), a number of significant developments were proposed, each of which has implications for quality issues and which you may have (or will have) experience. These included:

- '[The introduction of] Early Years Teachers to build upon the strengths of the Early Years Professionals programme, [specialising] in early childhood development and meet the same entry requirements and pass the same skills tests as trainee school teachers . . . people will train at Level 3 [that is, after GCSE exams, in England and Wales] to become Early Years Educators . . . they will often act as assistants to Early Years Teachers.' (Department for Education, 2013, p. 7)
- 'High quality providers [will be able] to offer more places by allowing greater flexibility. That flexibility for nurseries should go hand in hand with higher quality, so providers will only be able to operate with more children per adult if they employ high quality staff.' (Department for Education, 2013, p. 8)
- 'We will give childminders more flexibility. They will still only be able to look after six children in total. However, we will increase the number of under-5s they can look after from three to four, and the number of under-1s they can look after from one to two.' (Department for Education, 2013, p. 9)

Other proposals in *More great childcare* included offering parents more choice by supporting a greater diversity of provision, subject to regulation and inspection processes, some of which were to be simplified.

What all of these changes mean is that working in early years settings involves providing and demonstrating high-quality education and care, not only because this is a good thing in itself, but because it is the basis on which greater flexibility and autonomy will be allowed; and also, potentially, dealing with almost constant change. As an early years teacher you will be expected to reflect on, demonstrate and develop your own practice, engage with and work with other stakeholders, be a 'practice leader' of other staff, and still continue to be 'warm, friendly and approachable'!

Conclusion/Reflection point 1.3

Before you move on to further chapters:

- Look back at the notes you have made in previous refection points. Try to identify 'why' you came about such reflections—were they based on what you 'know', what you have 'experienced', what related policy suggests is required of you, or because of what 'social norms' you expect? Perhaps share or discuss your reflections with someone else, what differences are there, and what might the reasons for them be?

Now think about who early years is actually for. Your immediate answer is likely to be 'for the child, of course' but children are not the only beneficiaries of good-quality early years provision in the broader sense. Primary schools could be argued as 'benefiting' from receiving children who are 'school ready'. Some parents benefit from 'Childcare Tax Credit' that enables them to afford childcare and return to work. Governments in turn 'benefit' from working parents both in terms of taxes paid and a reduction in the welfare bill (although tax credits might be termed as a welfare benefit, it is frequently the case that this is far less of a cost on the national purse than unemployment benefits). Furthermore, there are strong links made between educational attainment and growth in economy, so again— who really is the ultimate beneficiary here? Now consider how this might bring about different measures of quality. Considering the three stakeholders: children, parents and government, how might their perspectives each shape what they consider to be 'quality' in early years?

References

Arnett, J. (1989). Caregivers in day-care centers: Does training matter? *Journal of Applied Developmental Psychology, 10*(4), 541–552.

Colwell, N., Gordon, R. A., Fujimoto, K., Kaestner, R., & Korenman, S. (2013). New evidence on the validity of the Arnett Caregiver Interaction Scale: Results from the early childhood longitudinal study-birth cohort. *Early Child Res Q, 28*(2), 218–233.

Department for Education and Employment. (2000). *Curriculum guidance for the foundation stage*. London: DFEE.

Department for Education. (2012a). *Foundations for quality: The independent review of early education and childcare qualifications (Nutbrown Report)*. London: DfE.

Department for Education. (2012b). *Statutory framework for the Early Years Foundation Stage*. DfE.

Department for Education. (2013). *More great childcare: Raising quality and giving parents more choice*. London: DfE.

Department for Education. (2014a). *Statutory framework for the Early Years Foundation Stage*. London: DfE.

Department for Education. (2014b). *Childcare and early years providers survey: 2013, TNS BMRB Report JN 117328*. London: DfE.

Department for Education and Skills. (2002). *Birth to three matters*. London: DfES.

Department for Education and Skills. (2006). *Children's workforce strategy: Building a world-class workforce for children, young people and families. The government's response to the consultation*. Nottingham: DfES.

Faux, K. (2012). *EYPS and the Nutbrown Review: Threat or opportunity?* Retrieved from http://www.nurseryworld.co.uk/nursery-world/news/1097199/eyps-nutbrown-review-threat-opportunity

Hadfield, M., Jopling, M., Needham, M., Waller, T., Coleyshaw, L., Emira, M., & K., R. (2012). *Longitudinal Study of Early Years Professional Status: An Exploration of Progress, Leadership and impact: Final Report*. London: Department for Education (DfE) and CeDARE, University of Wolverhampton.

Harms, T., Clifford, R., & Cryer, D. (2005). *Early Childhood Environment Rating Scale—Revised Edition*. New York, NY: Teachers College Press.

Harms, T., Cryer, D., & Clifford, R. (2006). *Infant/Toddler Environment Rating Scale—Revised Edition*. New York, NY: Teachers College Press.

Harms, T., Cryer, D., & Clifford, R. (2007). *Family Child Care Environment Rating Scale—Revised edition*. New York, NY: Teachers College Press.

Harms, T., Jacobs, E., & White, D. (2013). *School Age Care Environment Rating Scale—Updated Edition*. New York, NY: Teachers College Press.

Mathers, S., Singler, R., & Karemaker, A. (2012). *Improving quality in the early years: A comparison of perspectives and measures*. Oxford: A Plus, Daycare Trust and University of Oxford.

Moyles, J., Adams, S., & Musgrove, A. (2002). *SPEEL: Study of pedagogical effectiveness in early learning*. London: Department for Education and Skills (DfES).

National Childrens Bureau. (2013). *Quality improvement principles*. London: NCB.

NICHD Early Child Care Research Network. (2002). Child-care structure-process-outcome: direct and indirect effects of child-care quality on young children's development. *Psychological Science, 13*(3), 199–206.

Sammons, P., Taggart, B., Smees, R., Sylva, K., Melhuish, E., Siraj-Blatchford, I., & Elliot, K. (2003). *The Early Years Transition and Special Educational Needs (EYTSEN) Project.* London: Department for Education and Skills (DfES).

Siraj-Blatchford, I., Sylva, K., Muttock, K., Gilden, R., & Bell, D. (2002). *Researching effective pedagogy in the early years.* London: Department of Education and Skills (DfES).

Siraj-Blatchford, I., & Wong, Y. (1999). *Defining and evaluating 'quality' early childhood education in an international context: Dilemmas and possibilities.* London: Routledge.

Sylva, K., Melhuish, E., Sammons, P., Siraj-Blatchford, I., & Taggart, B. (2004). *The Effective Provision of Pre-school Education (EPPE) Project: Final Report. A longitudinal Study Funded by the DfES 1997–2004.* London: Department for Education and Skills (DfES).

Sylva, K., Siraj-Blatchford, I., & Taggart, B. (2010). *ECERS-E: The Early Childhood Environment Rating Scale Curricular Extension to ECERS-R* (3rd ed.). Stoke-on-Trent: Trentham Book.

The Children's Partnership. (undated). *EYFS statutory framework.* Retrieved from http://www.foundationyears.org.uk/eyfs-statutory-framework/

United Nations General Assembly. (1989). *Convention on the Rights of the Child, November 20, 1989.* United Nations Treaty Series, Vol. 1577.

United Nations Children's Fund (2000). *Defining quality in education.* Proceedings of The International Working Group on Education, Florence, Italy.

United Nations Children's Fund. (2010). *Child-friendly schools.* Retrieved June 1, 2015, from http://www.unicef.org/education/index_focus_schools.html

United Nations Children's Fund. (2011). *School readiness.* Retrieved June 1, 2015, from http://www.unicef.org/education/index_44888.html

2 Quality experiences for babies and very young children

Sarah Cousins and Perry Knight

Education of babies?

When we are thinking about babies and very young children, it is impossible to separate the concepts of care and education. While caring for babies and very young children, quality early years practitioners communicate with them through touch, facial expressions, playful talk, song and physical movements. Babies perceive this loving communication through all of their senses, and thereby learn to trust other people, gain self-esteem, become motivated to communicate, engage in play and grow in self-confidence.

This chapter emphasizes the importance of love for babies and very young children. First, attachment theory is explored, as is the importance of seamless provision between the home, education and care setting. This is followed by a consideration of what quality professionals do, how they behave and organize their environments to support the learning and development of babies and very young children. In the final sections, the importance of offering quality support for professionals working with babies and very young children is discussed. This support is required to ensure that all concerned, namely babies, very young children, parents and practitioners experience quality in partnership with each other.

What does high-quality education and care of babies and very young children mean?

The UK government policy in the twenty-first century has challenged the concept of early childcare. On the one hand, it seeks to incentivize and promote good parenting by giving families a choice to return to work when their child is at a young age. On the other hand, for some families a return to work is a means to ensure financial security and minimize daily pressures that a single household income may generate. Regardless of parents' reasons for returning to work, research has identified that early exposure to good-quality childcare will foster children's learning and enhance life chances, and that inadequate early childcare may leave a child 'at risk' of troubled relationships in later life (Page, 2011).

Fraenkel (2003) identifies high-quality care of very young children as involving a healthy and safe environment combined with education and social stimulation appropriate to the age and development of the child. This depends, in turn, on what carers offer to the young child and how they actively involve parents within the setting. Phillips and Adams (2001) highlight the importance of 'responsive' carers who offer developmental language, warmth, positivity, love and secure attachments.

Quality can be best defined in terms of the holistic development of babies and very young children in a family-centred environment. Murray (2014) characterizes such an environment as having a high staff to baby ratio, good staff training and high rates of pay, which lead to high staff morale, a sense of professionalism and a low staff turnover. Therefore, quality goes beyond the physical environment that is provided and is also dependent on staffing, qualifications and experience in promoting the best outcomes for babies (Wortham, 2006). Quality care for babies not only requires consistency of staffing, but also lasting relationships with parents. These relationships with parents go beyond the reporting of significant milestones, including those relating to physical, linguistic, cognitive, social and emotional development: they must involve a partnership with parents based on the provision of love and security.

This chapter sets out to explore high-quality care and education of babies and very young children in early years settings. Concepts of early childcare in which quality is defined purely through the family's experience of the setting are challenged. Instead, we emphasize the importance of family and stakeholder partnerships in which babies and very young children are able to freely transition between homes and early years settings. High-quality care and education, in this context, is applied to settings where babies and very young children are safe and secure, and in which high-quality professionals nurture a healthy development. This chapter explores the loving relationship between professionals and babies and very young children. Love, in this context, is expressed through hugs, cuddles and eye contact, and is evident in the provision of a stimulating environment and respect of individuality of every baby and very young child.

Attachment

Child development studies suggest that attachment within early years is demonstrated when children form significant and lasting relationships with family, particularly with the mother (Bowlby, 1958; Cassidy, 2008; Piaget, 1970). Despite parents having a great deal of control during early childhood, research suggests that young children have the ability to begin to develop clear preferences for other adults and playmates. In addition, settings offer babies and very young children the opportunities to develop within a broader context from their home, thus potentially helping them to build a greater awareness of themselves and others. Therefore, this notion raises the question of whether a baby or very young child has the ability to change their own behaviours for learning when they transfer between two discrete systems of home and setting. If attachment theory identifies boundaries in which a young child seeks stability and security, then that same child has the ability to form and select multiple attachments between a variety of carers.

Figure 2.1 illustrates layers of attachments required by young children in order to participate effectively and 'grow' within changing social situations. Its core signifies the stability of attachment between the child and immediate family, which Piaget (1970) identified as the bond between mother and child. Throughout early childhood, immediate family attachments develop through relationships of second-generation family members, thus classified as secondary attachment figures. As the child matures through each stage of development, there is greater focus on child–child interaction, rather than child–adult interaction dictated by experience with social setting, social experiences and self-regulated behaviour. The child's setting represents a holistic approach to successful attachment offering a range of child–adult and child–child relations. Yet for learning and development to be successful, the young child needs to negotiate and communicate in a

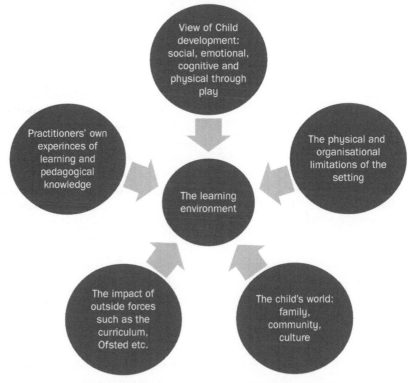

Figure 2.1 A conceptualization of development of attachment during early childhood

variety of contexts and within attachments that are removed from the immediate family setting.

Traditionally, from birth the mother–child attachment is an exclusive relationship (Gonzales-Mena, 2010). The relationship is founded on the need to provide love, warmth, food and security. Such a foundation is identified in Maslow's theory of motivation in which these qualities and need form the basis of his hierarchical structure (Maslow, 1954). At birth, research identifies that a newly born child can recognize their mother through her speech, smell and touch (Robinson, 2008). These senses forge an intense relationship in which complex emotions signify a lasting bond between the maternal carer and child. It is important to further consider whether such exclusivity can inhibit a very young child developing further multiple attachments within early years settings. Bowlby (2007) questions whether a child 'terminates' their attachment by seeking different forms of non-parental day care. Therefore, quality early childcare must provide protective factors in which a baby and their parents feel safe and secure within the setting (Gonzales-Mena, 2010). It is essential for early childcare to be family-centred whereby the needs of babies and very young children as well as the needs of their families are identified and met.

Transition into early childcare

Murray (2014) considers the range of complex feelings and concerns parents face when their young child enters day care. The attachment is not 'terminated' on entry to an early years setting, but rather enhanced allowing a baby to socialize and engage in a variety of activities with professionals and other children. The notion of separation anxiety between parent and baby can be minimized by carefully planned transition into the setting. Transitions are potentially stressful periods not only for babies and very young children, but also for their parents and anxiety can have detrimental long-term effect for children and their parents. Therefore, when discussing quality, the notion of attachment needs to consider strategies of how both the provider and parents work in partnership to support a young child entering day care.

Murray (2014) further identifies gradual transitions as essential. This is when the parents are initially actively involved within the setting, and the setting is actively involved with home visits, with the intention of developing an individualized care plan for the baby. It is important that the setting has a full history of the child, knows their daytime patterns, comforters and soothers. For example, a quality setting will encourage a baby or very young child to eat and sleep according to their own established pattern. As transition progresses, parental involvement will gradually decrease when both feel at ease. The baby will begin to identify with attachments associated with both home and early years setting.

Vignette: Transitions into an early years setting

Anne cares for 9 babies, aged 3 to 18 months, in her setting. The baby room is divided into a sleeping and activity area. Crawlers and toddlers can move between areas with ease. The baby room has a vast range of natural product resources, which are readily accessible. Recently, Anne has been supporting a family with the transition of their first baby into her setting.

It is very important for parents to choose the right setting for their child and this was not confirmed on their first visit. Anne identified different times across different days in which they could visit. To gain as much information on the baby, each visit involved a conversation with Anne and the proposed key person. On the fourth and final pre-visit, mother, baby and key person spend time together in the baby room with both playing with the baby with a toy from home. After this visit, a transition plan is discussed and put in place for the baby and their family. The plan involves:

- Three home visits by the key person during different times of the day. These are used for the key person to develop a relationship with the key person, and for the key person to be with the baby in familiar surroundings.
- The baby's first few sessions in the baby room is accompanied by their mother. During this visit the mother and the key person worked with the baby. However, at points the mother leaves the baby room for short periods to speak with Anne.

After these sessions, the mother leaves her baby for longer periods until the baby's first full session on their own. The family now has a consistent routine in which one parent drops off their baby and collects them at the end of the session. The baby is very content at the setting and is meeting developmental outcomes. The partnership between the setting and family is strong due to the transition and time taken to welcome the family to the baby room.

Transitions are about change: they are passages from one experience to another. This can be further defined in early childcare as either a baby's physical stage, learning development or activity in which the baby participates. Merrill and Britt (2008) discuss transitions as physical and outside forces: physical forces consider challenges to learning as a baby develops from sitting, to crawling and to walking. Each new challenge requires different learning tools. For example, prior to crawling, babies learn from vocalized sound, sensory stimulation and floor toys. They require transitioning to each activity by their carer and practitioner to maximize enjoyment of learning opportunities and seek further learning challenges. This is achieved by linking each activity through thoughtful preparation, practitioner speech and resource. Quality care and learning involves observation, consideration and analysis: the early years professional then needs to consider the best approach to a very young child's learning (Elliot, 2003). This is essential in providing an environment in which different relationships are formed and in which babies and very young children develop multiple attachments through carefully managed transitions to new learning and different relationships.

The importance of love in quality settings

Practitioners become babies' 'companions' while they are in settings: these practitioner-companions are 'the people who give [babies] companionable attention, and to whom they are bound by love or affection' (Roberts, 2010, p. 56). As early as the 1950s, Gardner (1956) made numerous references to the importance of love in early years education. She wrote that a child 'often shows very marked improvement, in many and often unexpected ways, once he is convinced that he is really loved and is able to give pleasure by his presence' (Gardner, 1956, p. 19). Gardner goes on to use the term 'loved people' (1956, p. 20) to describe the adults who cared for very young children in nurseries. While she wrote that these 'loved people' were of less profound importance to a child's feelings than their own parents, she also emphasized that children learn that they can share these loved people without losing their love.

From these perspectives across two centuries then, there is a place for love in professional work with babies and very young children. Page and Elfer (2013) report that parents want practitioners to love their children in settings and, according to Cousins (2015), practitioners say it is important for them to love the babies and very young children they care for. Gerhardt (2004) stresses the importance of love based on her experience and knowledge as a psychoanalytic psychotherapist. She presents the case for love from a biological perspective, arguing that people's psychological make-up is, to a significant extent, shaped in relation to their formative experience of being loved, or not. In a reference to work by Bowlby (1988), Gerhardt demonstrates that there is a direct correlation between feeling loved by particular others as young children and becoming emotionally balanced for life.

In an action research study about quality provision in Children's Centres, Manning-Morton and Thorp (2003) argue that children do not thrive if they do not also receive loving attention. They point to the somatosensory system in children's brains, which is stimulated from birth through touch and emphasize that young children internalize the way they are touched and held, and that 'this becomes part of their sense of self' (Manning-Morton & Thorp, 2015, p. 45). Loving young children does involve touching in the form of holding and hugging.

This developmental perspective on the importance of love as something that is internalized in the physical body from an early age also suggests that it pays dividends through life. The provision of love should be seen as an essential part of the quality role of baby room practitioners.

Quality practitioners who care for babies and very young children

The word 'care' is also frequently applied in early years research and the term 'ethic of care' is used to talk about how people apply their experiences of caring and being cared for in their work as carers. It is important, in the first instance, to consider the word 'care', as distinct from 'love'; then we will consider what is meant by an 'ethic of care'.

The *Collins' English Dictionary* offers several definitions of the verb 'to care', including 'To be troubled or concerned; to be affected emotionally' and 'To provide physical needs or help or comfort for'. 'To care' then is not the same as 'to love' because, according to the second definition, it is about the actions associated with attending to someone's physical and emotional needs. Additionally, someone might *care* for another person; perhaps even in a loving way, but not necessarily *love* them. However, although care is more about duty and the actions that need to be taken to meet other people's needs, it is necessarily enacted within relationships (Lynch, Baker, & Lyons, 2009) and these relationships may sometimes involve love. Indeed, the first definition implies that carers may feel emotional in relation to the object of their care. Additionally, early years practitioners may need to call on their inner selves to fulfil their duties of care. Osgood argues that for the women in her early years study, '"a caring self" was intrinsic to their subjective identity formation' (Osgood, 2012, p. 139). In other words, being caring was how the practitioners perceived themselves, and how they presented themselves to the world.

The philosopher of education, Nel Noddings, has proposed in a series of books and articles that, in non-familial contexts, people need to act ethically out of a sense of duty. In such contexts, she argued that people refer to an 'ethic of care' to guide their actions until these become habitual and natural. She argued that people care for others in response to their very human, present needs and demands, and she proposed that such an 'ethic of care' binds carers and cared-fors. From Noddings' perspective, then, practitioners and the children they care for enter into binding relationships that feel comfortable and have their own regular patterns and unique features.

Goldstein (1998) applied Noddings' notion of 'ethic of care' to her narrative study of a teacher, concluding that caring for children is an intellectual as well as an emotional act. She proposed that caring, which she associated with love, was 'an action rather than an attribute, a deliberate moral and intellectual stance rather than simply a feeling' (Goldstein 1998, p. 259).

Goldstein's and Noddings' notion of 'ethic of care', then, supports other notions of quality in the sense that it is a conscious disposition, adopted in professional contexts to enhance the experience of babies and young children in settings. However, it also complicates the notion of quality since it relies on specific relationships that grow between carers and cared-fors and so is less predictable and reliable: it is dependent on the natural and learned dispositions of baby-room practitioners.

Quality work with babies and very young children is carried out by people who do, think and feel, and who draw on their personal subjectivities as they strive to achieve a 'culture of care characterised by affectivity, altruism, self-sacrifice and conscientiousness' (Osgood, 2012, p. 131). These acts of care involve encounters with other people, are reciprocal, social and non-hierarchical.

Reflection point 2.1

Consider how the notion of 'ethic of care' aligns with the notion of quality put forward in the Early Years Foundation Stage (EYFS).

- What are the similarities and differences?
- What are some of the potential difficulties with such a notion in professional contexts? For example, how can 'ethic of care' be measured?
- How can leaders and managers report on the impact of adopting an 'ethic of care' in their settings?

Constant love and care for babies and very young children

Elfer, Goldschmied, and Selleck (2012) argue that quality settings for babies and very young children should be like their own homes, with one key person responsible for each child. This key person acts like a parent in the setting, carrying out all the caring and educating work with each child. The key person, then, not only engages in one-to-one play with their key children, but also changes their nappies, soothes them to sleep, supports them to feed themselves, watches them eat, gets to know them well and enters into a relationship with them.

Reflection point 2.2

Do baby rooms need to be like children's own homes? Should they be understood as extensions of the home with a small number of adults caring constantly for each baby or very young child?

- What sources do you draw on to reach this view?
- What are some of the challenges that leaders face in attempting to replicate the home?

Quality practitioners with specific knowledge and skills for work with babies

Quality care and education calls for not only highly skilled and knowledgeable practitioners, but also warm, sensitive and resilient practitioners. Some researchers have argued that the quality of this work with babies and very young children is dependent on the social and emotional well-being of early years practitioners (Elfer et al., 2012; Manning-Morton & Thorp, 2015). Furthermore, Manning-Morton (2006) has argued that work with babies and very young children requires practitioners who not only have a deep understanding of the children they care for but also of themselves as people. Quality early years practitioners need to know who they are and have reflected on their own histories. They are people who will be able to step back from situations, and act professionally at all times rather than purely intuitively.

That is not to say that intuition and knowledge that is gained through living in the world is not important. It is also a valuable form of knowledge that may be applied to the work of early years practitioners. As Manning-Morton and Thorp articulated, however, early years practitioners should be able to 'temper their responses' to different situations as they arise (2015, p. 137). To do this, they will need to draw on their professional knowledge and understanding of child development as well as their experience as continuously developing professionals.

Reflection point 2.3

Manning-Morton and Thorp suggest that 'The positive contribution of early years provision to the social and emotional well-being of children is critically dependent on the social and emotional well-being of early years practitioners' (2015, p. 141).

- Do you agree with this statement?
- What resources might you draw on to ensure your own social and emotional well-being, if this is, as suggested here, so important?
- What arguments, if any, can you think of that support a contrasting position?

Quality practitioners: carers, teachers or both?

This chapter has emphasized the importance of caring and loving relationships between practitioners and babies in settings. How do these qualities support *learning*? How do quality practitioners *educate* babies and very young children? It is important to be aware that learning cannot take place unless babies and very young children are well cared for, with all their physical and emotional needs consistently and well met. If babies are well fed, comfortable, well-rested and generally well attended to by one or two main carers with a real interest in them, then they will get on with all the things babies are competent to do. They will learn about the world and their place in it, how to communicate, manipulate objects, test out how things work, observe what happens, play with sounds, gain physical strength to do things, move in different ways and be playful. Learning occurs in relationships with skilful and knowledgeable adults that babies and very young children can depend on.

A play-based curriculum, as will be discussed in Chapter 7 of this book, requires effective learning to be self-chosen and self-directed (Stacey, 2009). Babies are playful from their earliest days and so quality practitioners also need to know how to support children's play. While national priorities may emphasize the value of play in supporting specific areas of the curriculum, such as literacy or numeracy (Wood, 2013), quality early years practitioners know that there are different types of play that babies engage in, including discovery play, play to test things out and exploratory play. All of these are important in supporting the learning and development of babies and very young children.

As stated in the introduction to this chapter, it is impossible to separate the care and education of babies and very young children. If babies and very young children are well cared for, then they are free to learn since they are, according to the *birth to three matters* framework, 'competent learners from birth'. This framework is no longer current, but is still widely referred to, and much of its content is incorporated within the EYFS (Department for Education, 2014). The framework points to the importance of strong relationships between babies and adults they can depend on and states that babies and young children learn most effectively when, with the support of knowledgeable and trusted adults, they are:

> actively involved and interested
>
> given appropriate responsibility
>
> allowed to make errors, decisions and choices, and
>
> respected as autonomous and competent learners. (Department for Education and Skills, 2002, p. 5)

Such work calls for quality practitioners who are skilful, knowledgeable, dependable, committed and willing to enter into extended relationships with babies and their families.

There is no contradiction, then, between caring and teaching in quality care and education of babies and very young children. Indeed, the Office for Standards in Education, Children's Services and Skills (Ofsted) offered a wide definition of teaching in the context of early years. Inspectors were asked to find out about the quality of teaching by observing:

> Children at play
>
> The interactions between practitioners and children
>
> Care routines and how they are used to support children's personal development. (Office for Standards in Education, Children's Services and Skills, 2015)

Play is an opportunity for babies and very young children to learn how to interact with others: be playful; to find out how things work; express themselves freely; enjoy their interactions with others; and gain in self-confidence. Similarly, every interaction babies and very young children have with trusted, dependable adults are opportunities for them to develop as communicators, gain confidence to express themselves and be creative with language. Care routines, well carried out by loving and dependable adults, are seen as opportunities for teaching babies and very young children that they can trust others, and supporting them to feel confident and safe, and develop independence.

Reflection point 2.4

Observe a practitioner at play with a baby or very young child. Identify how they are teaching them through:

- play
- their interactions with the babies and very young children
- carrying out care routines

Quality support for practitioners who work with babies

The kind of practice we have described requires specific skills and knowledge, draws on intuition and professionalism, and also involves love: this is, therefore, highly complex and multi-faceted. The work is at once personal and professional, emotional and cerebral. There is perhaps a need, as proposed by Page and Elfer (2013), for more awareness about this complexity and the challenges it brings. It is possible that some practitioners, for example, may form attachments with particular babies, feel a sense of loss when their children move on to different rooms, be unable to talk freely about affective matters in the baby room, or be worried about touching babies and very young children as a sign of love.

One form of support is to provide opportunities for early years practitioners working with babies and very young children to reflect on their own practice. Manning-Morton emphasizes the importance of practitioners developing as mature, emotionally intelligent, self-aware adults, and 'becom[ing] experts in themselves' (2006, p. 45) She recommends that practitioners receive high levels of support in order to meet day-to-day challenges, including instances when they may be rejected by children, and emphasizes that work with very young children involves practitioners' hearts as much as their minds.

Similarly, Osgood argues that practitioners need improved support for this complex work. She suggests this from the point of view of mitigating the human cost of this 'emotionally demanding work' (Osgood, 2012, p. 131) and proposes that if early years practitioners were allowed to draw on their 'life experience and wisdom' as indicated within her concept of 'professionalism from within', they might develop an even 'deeper-level appreciation for the work (i.e. professionalism)' (Osgood, 2012, p. 130).

Page and Elfer (2013) note that teachers often adopt an intuitive approach in their daily work and 'draw . . . on personal experience rather than a body of theoretical knowledge' (2013, p. 564). They propose that managers should facilitate opportunities for staff to talk about complex aspects of their work, and allow issues to be brought into the open. Managers, they propose, should establish a climate in which it is acceptable for there to be no clear answers to questions, problems and issues may be raised, uncertainty can prevail, and practitioners are able to talk about their feelings and concerns.

This emphasis on the need for reflective talk was applied in research by Goouch and Powell (2012) who set up a project for baby-room practitioners. This was in response to practitioners' stated need for 'specific development opportunities' and their sense of feeling 'poorly supported' in their work with babies (2012, pp. 81–82). They found that the baby-room practitioners were very willing to engage in the project and learn from each other. These critical spaces for talking and thinking helped the practitioners 'to develop a sense of their own worth in their work and to develop a "voice"' (2012, p. 84), and also helped them to think about their practice and gain a better understanding about their work with babies and very young children. The primary importance of this research was in exploring the value of creating quality spaces for baby-room practitioners to engage in 'professional talk' (2012, p. 84). These opportunities for talk helped the participants in their research to interpret their experiences in the baby room, value particular aspects of their work, make links with their own life experiences, reflect, think about their practice and consider other possibilities. 'Talk through narrative constructions', they found, was a powerful learning experience (2012, p. 85).

The complexity of the role of early years practitioners, then, is widely written about, as is the importance of loving children in professional contexts. However, many of the sources we have drawn on here agree that these complexities are often unspoken and unacknowledged. Page (2011), for example, found that there was a need, in her conceptualization of 'professional love', for a language of love to be developed through which to explore this complex work; Osgood (2012) calls for more space to be made for people to draw on their subjective experiences to enhance their professional practice; and Goouch and Powell (2012) emphasize the value of space to talk.

Conclusion: quality experiences for babies and young children

This chapter draws on the notion that a quality experience for babies and very young children is founded on secure attachments and love. It is necessary to recognize that the developing child moves between a complex social system of a loving family unit, to the complexities of the baby room. Therefore, to ensure quality and sustainability of care and love between each social system, the complexities of relationships should be contained within the microsystems of the immediate family and baby, and the key person and baby. All adults working with babies and very young children are brought together through their identification with the child. Quality is defined as love and attachment providing a firm foundation for a baby or very young child, thus helping them to develop and thrive between these closely interlinked environments.

References

Bowlby, J. (1958). The nature of the child's tie to his mother. *International Journal of PsychoAnalysis, 39,* 350–373.

Bowlby, J. (1988). *A secure base: Clinical applications of attachment theory.* Abingdon: Routledge.

Bowlby, R. (2007). Babies and toddlers in non-parental daycare can avoid stress and anxiety if they can develop a lasting secondary attachment bond with one carer who is consistently accessible to them. *Attachment and Human Development, 9*(4), 307–319.

Cassidy, J. (2008). The nature of the child's ties. In J. Cassidy & P. R. Shaver (Eds.), *Handbook of attachment: Theory, research and clinical applications* (2nd ed., pp. 3–22). New York: Guilford Press.

Cousins, S. (2015). *Practitioners' constructions of love in the context of early childhood education and care: A narrative inquiry.* University of Sheffield.

Department for Education. (2014). *Statutory framework for the Early Years Foundation Stage.* London: DfE.

Department for Education and Skills. (2002). *Birth to three matters.* London: DfES.

Elfer, P., Goldschmied, E., & Selleck, D. Y. (2012). *Key persons in the early years: Building relationships for quality provision in early years settings and primary schools* (2nd ed.). Abingdon: Routledge.

Elliot, E. (2003). *Challenging our assumptions: Helping a baby adjust to center care.* Washington DC: NAEYC Publications.

Fraenkel, P. (2003). Contemporary two-parent families. In F. Walsh (Ed.), *Normal family processes* (3rd ed.). New York: Guilford Press.

Gardner, D. (1956). *The education of young children.* London: Methuen.

Gerhardt, S. (2004). *Why love matters: How affection shapes a baby's brain.* London: Routledge.

Goldstein, L. (1998). More than gentle smiles and warm hugs: Applying the ethic of care to early childhood education. *Journal of Research in Childhood Education, 12*(2), 244–261.

Gonzales-Mena, J. (2010). *Child, family and community: Family centred early care and education* (6th ed.). Harlow: Pearson/Prentice Hall.

Goouch, K., & Powell, S. (2012). Orchestrating professional development for baby room practitioners: raising the stakes in new dialogic encounters. *Journal of Early Childhood Research, 11*(1), 78–92.

Lynch, K., Baker, J., & Lyons, M. (2009). *Affective equality: Love, Care and injustice.* Basingstoke: Routledge.

Manning-Morton, J. (2006). The personal is professional: Professionalism and the birth to threes practitioner. *Contemporary Issues in Early Childhood, 7*(1), 42–52.

Manning-Morton, J., & Thorp, M. (2003). *Key times for play: The first three years.* Maidenhead: Open University Press.

Manning-Morton, J., & Thorp, M. (2015). *Two-year-olds in early years settings: Journeys of discovery.* Maidenhead: Open University Press.

Maslow, A. (1954). *Motivation and personality.* New York: Harper.

Merrill, S., & Britt, D. (2008). Helping babies make transitions. *Young Children, 63*(3), 60–62.

Murray, L. (2014). *The psychology of babies: How relationships support development from birth to two.* London: Constable Robinson.

Office for Standards in Education, Children's Services and Skills. (2015). *Early years inspection handbook.* London: Ofsted.

Osgood, J. (2012). *Narratives from the nursery.* London: Routledge.

Page, J., & Elfer, P. (2013). The emotional complexity of attachment interactions in nursery. *European Early Childhood Education Research Journal, 21*(4), 553–567.

Page, J. (2011). Do mothers want professional carers to love their babies? *Journal of Early Childhood Research, 1*(14), 1–14.

Phillips, D., & Adams, G. (2001). Child care and our youngest children. *Future Child, 11*(1), 34–51.

Piaget, J. (1970). Carmichael's manual of child psychology (Volume 1). In P. H. Mussen (3rd ed., pp. 703–732). New York: Wiley.

Roberts, R. (2010). *Wellbeing from birth.* London: Sage.

Robinson, M. (2008). *Child development 0–8: A journey through the early years.* Maidenhead: Open University Press.

Stacey, S. (2009). *Emergent curriculum in early childhood settings: From theory to practice.* St. Paul, MN: Red Leaf Press.

Wood, E. (2013). *Play, learning and the early childhood curriculum* (3rd ed.). London: Sage.

Wortham, S. (2006). *Learning identity: The Joint emergence of social identification and academic learning.* Cambridge: Cambridge University Press.

3 Quality early years environments

Abigail Gosling

In Chapter 1, we described how difficult it is to define quality and one aspect of this complexity stems from the challenges we face when we try to define, describe or evaluate environments for learning. While instruments like the Early Childhood Environment Rating Scale (ECERS), (Harms, Clifford, and Cryer, 2005) suggest observable measures and allow comparison across settings and contexts, they do not always provide an insight into the 'fine-grained' detail of how environments support or constrain learning, interaction, or social and emotional development. They also do not fully capture the aspects of an environment that, as we have seen, are so important for parents and carers: security, warmth and safety.

High-quality environments, then, are those that support all aspects of a child's development:

- *Cognitive development*: by encouraging them to explore and learn about what is around them, and to think creatively.
- *Social development*: by fostering the ability to communicate and socialize with others.
- *Emotional development*: by helping children to regulate their feelings, feel safe and secure.
- *Physical development*: by supporting their fine and gross motor skills, coordination and health.

Early years settings are many and varied: from 'pack away' provision in a church hall, which requires all the learning resources to be dismantled at the end of the day, to a bespoke Children's Centre that may have multi-user rooms; and from a day nursery in a nineteenth-century house with features such as stairs and many small rooms to negotiate, to a reception class in a former junior school whose buildings were designed with different ages of children, and different ideas about teaching and learning in mind. The physical features of each setting may have a significant impact on the extent to which early years practitioners can create the quality environment they envisage, and in some cases this can provide real challenges. Nevertheless, each unique setting can be developed to provide a quality environment in which the children can learn and develop in all the ways listed above.

Adults also need to be aware that they bring preconceptions, ideas and intentions to their work whether they are consciously aware of it or not. The environment they create each day can be considered to be relational, reflecting their beliefs, cultural experiences and the world they inhabit every day. The well-known *Reggio Emilia* schools in Italy are a good example: their design, and the activities they enable, reflects the broader cultural concerns and practices of the commune in which they are located (Edwards, Gandini, & Forman, 1998; Malaguzzi, 1993). These spaces deliberately mirror the sociocultural—relational principles that underpin the Reggio Emilia approach. There are spaces to talk, debate and discuss, and spaces for children to represent their thinking in the many different languages available to them, through dance, sculpture, paint and music. The architectural design of the educational settings reflects Italian cityscapes and community with their interconnected spaces and meeting points designed to promote a particular way of learning for the children in the settings (Ceppi & Zini, 1998).

In short, the development of a rich, high-quality early years environment will be influenced by an intricate web of interconnected beliefs and experiences that affect the way practitioners think about the children in their care. The environments in which they choose to work, or which they develop themselves, will reflect practitioners' views of what is valued in childhood, the cultural setting, which may, in turn, have impacted on their personal experiences of learning as a child. These will then be complicated further by their experiences of training and practice (which may itself reflect particular ideas about children, teaching and learning); and their understandings of the different theories of how children learn (Brownlee & Berthelsen, 2006). It is, therefore, important to reflect consciously on your own particular view on quality environments and how it shapes practice.

Children's learning and quality environments

Children learn through actively engaging first hand with their environment, and from interacting with their peers and supportive adults within it. We know that children develop at varying rates; that their experiences influence their learning (Rogoff, 2003); and that children need to be supported to develop self-regulatory skills alongside cognitive skills (Bodrova & Leong, 2005). These insights lead us to think about providing environments that enable these interactions and experiences, and that encourage autonomy and enquiry. Guidance on the Early Years Foundation Stage (EYFS) encourages practitioners to provide 'enabling environments [that offer] stimulating resources, relevant to all the children's cultures and communities, rich learning opportunities through play and playful teaching, and support for children to take risks and explore' (Early Education, 2012, p. 21). The characteristics of effective learning in the EYFS (Early Education, 2012) directs us to provide an environment that is open for children to play, explore and think creatively about the experiences they are engaged in.

These ideas align closely with Vygotsky's ideas on learning as socially mediated (Vygotsky, 1978) and reinforce the importance of the role of more knowledgeable others (usually setting up learning opportunities, providing support and 'tools' to help solve problems and offering formative feedback in the learning environment in order to 'make meaning'.) Adults can and should help to scaffold children's learning through sensitive, stimulating and challenging use of interaction as well as the provision of the resources and learning spaces. This way of thinking about learning is essentially social and the sustained, shared talking and thinking it enables is crucial in not only cognitive development but also supports communication, and social and emotional development as well.

The idea of the child as an apprentice in the learning environment, with adults and children co-constructing understandings, is important to bear in mind here (Rogoff, 1990). Rogoff sees development as taking place on three levels: on the individual cognitive level within the child; on the social level involving other people within the community; and finally on the sociocultural level whereby people 'engage in the processes of making and sharing meaning' (Rogoff, 2003, p. 32). This suggests that we need to envisage the learning environment as offering opportunities for co-operative and collaborative learning to take place, but also for new understandings to emerge for all participants. The social context is not just a 'container' in which learning takes place, but rather influences and is influenced by it.

At this sociocultural level, children's development is complex and we need to consider the diversity of learning in communities (Rogoff, 2003; Smidt, 2006). This involves thinking carefully about the child's experiences of family, taking account of the particular social and cultural context in which the setting is in and using that knowledge to create a relevant meaningful environment for learning. The Organization for Economic Co-operation and Development (OECD), in a review of early education across international contexts, emphasizes the need for children to learn in meaningful contexts, which is linked to their intrinsic motivation: what really matters and interests the children (OECD, 2010). However, practitioners need to be careful here: it is not enough just to introduce some resources or contextualize a task in a way that only superficially reflects the communities in which children live. Williams and De Gaetano (1985) encourage practitioners to move away from a superficial and tokenistic multicultural approach within the learning environment towards a position of 'cultural relevancy' where learning environments reflect children's lives, families and communities much more holistically and authentically. And, according to a broader sociocultural perspective, practitioners need to acknowledge that children's learning may have wider impacts beyond the immediate goals of a specific task or the location within which it occurs—it will contribute to the broader culture too.

There is, of course, a tension evident: while practitioners may be aware of these broader social and sociocultural aspects of young children's learning, and the advice given on how to plan and administer the EYFS seems to align with these, there is another view of learning that sees it as primarily individual and linear. This has had a considerable influence on the way educational institutions and curricula have developed, and it has shaped provision in the classroom, not least through the design of assessment activities. It can result in children being offered materials, spaces and activities that are seen to match their development too closely, thus offering little opportunity to challenge and excite growing minds. Nevertheless, it continues to influence the way learning environments are constructed, and activities are designed.

In some school settings we still see a rigid and linear approach to children's learning of early number concepts and operations that might dictate that nursery, reception or key stage 1 classes might have specific, separate sets of resources, on the assumption that children will pass through distinct stages in their mathematical understanding. It is more common in good quality early years settings to see a more flexible approach that involves allowing children to select resources and develop their own strategies, with the teacher 'scaffolding' learning, and introducing new objects, materials and concepts. The child develops a repertoire of approaches, as well as the self-regulatory abilities that will make them a more autonomous learner. The resources themselves must be open-ended and, therefore, offer the possibility for the child to differentiate how they use them according to their own particular level of development and interest. This is a theme to which we will return in Chapter 7, in which we discuss how quality can be understood in the curriculum.

Reflection point 3.1

- How might ideas about how children learn differ between policymakers, practitioners, parents and the children themselves?
- How might these different views be reflected in the physical nature of the learning environment?

Learning environments for social and emotional development

The previous section was concerned with children's learning—their cognitive development—but as we suggested in the introduction to this chapter, quality environments also contribute significantly to other aspects of their development as well. Chawla-Duggan suggests that the learning environment 'informs the development of the child via the emotional experience of that environment' (2011, p. 157). In other words, when a child is happy, safe and secure, cognitive challenges are more likely to be met and deeper level learning is much more likely to occur. The management of emotions (the 'self-regulation' we discussed in the previous section) also underpins other key skills for learning.

Whitebread (2012) describes how an effective learning environment in which cognitive challenge is promoted brings together a range of practices, informed by different theoretical perspectives of children's development and learning. You may have encountered these in your learning, possibly separately, but what is interesting here is that they all have some bearing on thinking about early years environments. There are four key elements:

- Emotional warmth, with high levels of involvement and a commitment to well-being and security—building on the work of Bowlby (1953) and Laevers (1994).

- Encouraging children to take control, where play is the main medium (Guha, 1987; Moyles, 2010).

- A view of learning as an active process of meaning-making and practices that foster this in young children, based on the constructivist theories of Piaget and Inhelder (1969) and Vygotsky (1978).

- The articulation of learning made explicit by adults to young children through sustained, shared conversations (Sylva, Melhuish, Sammons, Siraj-Blatchford, & Taggart, 2004).

The centrality of talk

We know that children learn both with and from others, and the constructivist and sociocultural perspectives we have already discussed argue that language is central to the co-construction of knowledge. Furthermore, the importance of sustained shared thinking and conversation has been identified as a key aspect of high-quality early learning environments (Sylva et al., 2004). This requires bi-directionality of interactions (Maccoby, 2007) so shared talk, including talk initiated by children, must be a key feature in the early years environment.

We need, therefore, to construct environments that promote speaking and listening—adults talking to and listening to children, children talking and listening to adults, and to other children. Jarman (2007) talks about communication-friendly spaces that are stimulating but not overly so, and within which there are cosy, small areas where children feel safe and able to initiate conversations and chat in privacy. This also means that opportunities for talk, including child-initiated talk and sustained talk between children, need to be recognized. For example, snack time, rather than simply being a quick refuelling stop can be reframed and organized as an opportunity for social interactions, child- and teacher-led talk (not necessarily just about the snacks themselves!) and informal news sharing, conversation and planning what we might do next.

There has been a growing awareness of the importance of consulting with children about their educational experience. This has been informed by the United Nations (UN) Convention on the Rights of the Child (United Nations General Assembly, 1989); however, consultation does not need to involve formal processes, although many people may assume that this involves school councils or surveys. In an early years setting, Clarke and Moss (2001) and the Organization for Economic Co-operation and Development (2012) have demonstrated both the potential and the impact of listening to children's views about their own learning, including their ideas on how to develop the best learning spaces to meet their needs. The EYFS recognizes the importance of building on children's voices, encouraging practitioners to listen to what the children are 'saying', either verbally, or through their many and varied ways of making visible their interests and preferences, and incorporate their ideas into the learning environment.

An environment that encourages this broader children's talk can, therefore, be developed further by engaging the children in thinking about the kinds of activities that they would like to take part in and the spaces in which they would like to interact, learn and play. For example, children in a maintained nursery school were particularly interested in dinosaurs and this was documented in practitioner observations, discussions with parents and carers and across the team. The children were asked to suggest how they would like to learn more about dinosaurs, and from their ideas the sandpit was recreated into a dinosaur world both indoors and outdoors. Non-fiction books were used by the children to help them to decide what resources to include in these areas and parents were encouraged to support the development by bringing in things from home too. Technology was incorporated through the use of iPads and the smartboard to research websites for further information and to recreate landscapes to compliment the physical resources. In this way, the children's interests and voices were integral to the development of the learning environment.

The importance of play

Play is an essential medium for children's learning and the quality learning environment must promote opportunities for children to engage in playful experiences. The EYFS frameworks have placed the child's learning within a play-based framework (Department for Children, Schools and Families, 2008; Department for Education, 2014; Early Education, 2012). The characteristics of effective learning in the Development Matters guidance (Early Education, 2012) champion play and exploration, active learning and creating and thinking critically as fundamental for cognitive development, and the environment needs to offer opportunities to facilitate them.

Vygotsky stresses the importance of play and in particular pretend play in the learning environment for developing imagination and abstract thought (1978). In play children are not set predetermined limits on their thinking: knowledge is being actively discovered. He argues that children engaged in play work at a higher intellectual level. Play, therefore, has a pivotal role in fostering learning across all dimensions of development in young children; furthermore, its role in increasing neural structures and as a means for developing lifelong learning skills is well documented (Isenberg and Quisenberry, 2002).

Environments for resilience and growth

The kinds of environment we are describing, designed to encourage children to engage in independent learning and to initiate and sustain talk, align well with the idea of children being not only self-regulating but also resilient: able to reflect, solve problems and not overly dependent on adults doing everything for them. In her studies of children's learning, Carol Dweck (2000) emphasizes the importance of children being given the opportunity to learn through their own efforts, seeing themselves as having ownership and mastery of their learning, and, therefore, seeing failure as a challenge. This means that learning activities and environments need to be designed so that they give children opportunities to persist in the face of problems until they eventually master the challenges they encounter. Technology areas, for example, need to allow children to experiment and adapt, to try using different materials to make things, and to make multiple versions of things, rather than being dependent on a teacher to 'get it right'. The role of the teacher is to set up a provocation to learn, provide resources, and sensitively intervene and support when appropriate, asking questions and offering advice rather than taking over and demonstrating the right way to do things.

A performance-focused environment, which is linked too closely to the production of objects or texts and which is driven by curriculum outcomes rather than the way children learn, is more likely to promote what Dweck calls 'learned helplessness' in children. This is accentuated by feedback that stresses ability rather than persistence, resilience or curiosity. When children in these environments are faced with a problem that they cannot solve, they do not have the confidence to try, and may justify this in terms of not being clever enough, they have learned to be 'helpless' unless another person, usually an adult, solves the problem for them. In the learning-focused environments that Dweck advocates, children are encouraged to believe that 'I can do this', developing a positive attitude and disposition to learning. Rather than learned helplessness, children develop a 'growth mindset', which progressively increases their confidence in their own ability to learn in the present and in the future, Claxton (2006) calls this 'learning power'. Developing what Dweck and Claxton would describe as the right dispositions in children demands that teachers think about how all aspects of their practice, including designing curricula and activities, giving feedback and advice, and organizing learning environments, will contribute not just to learning 'now' but in the future as well.

It may be helpful to draw together the different aspects discussed above in the form of a diagram (Figure 3.1) that identifies the factors that impact on the environment.

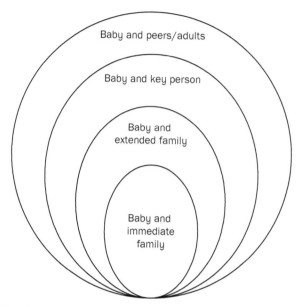

Figure 3.1 Possible influences on the development of a high-quality learning environment

Four types of learning environment

It is not the intention of this chapter to provide a blueprint on how to create a high-quality enabling environment because so much will depend on the context of the setting, including the physical features of the setting itself, the experiences of the children and practitioners who attend, their families and communities in which they live, and so on. Instead, it will aim to suggest the key elements that are required to shape the environment in order to provide a quality experience for young children.

Positive dispositions and attitudes to learning are key for learning and adults influence these responses through the kind of environment they create. Claxton and Carr (2004) bring together the elements we have discussed (organization, the role of talk and children's voice, the degree of autonomy and self-regulation that are allowed) and characterize four types of learning environment, each of which is also considered from the dispositions towards learning that they encourage (Table 3.1).

Table 3.1: Typology of Environments

Type of learning environment	Pedagogical approach	Characteristics	Child's perspective
A **prohibiting** environment	Tightly scheduled learning, adult-directed, children quickly move from one activity to another	Little time to persist, develop self-regulation, resilience or to collaborate. Child's voice not valued	I learn by doing what I am told and follow the adult lead
An **affording** environment	A balance between adult-and child-led learning, more relaxed routines, adult not maximizing learning through pedagogical approaches	Positive learning dispositions developing for some children. Child's voice less valued	I can learn with resources that are available in the setting
An **inviting** environment	A balance between child- and adult-led learning, with some elements of sustained, shared thinking and flexible routines	Positive learning dispositions developing for all children Child's voice valued	I can learn using resources independently and talk to adults and other children about what I am doing
A **potentiating** environment	Invite expressions of learning dispositions and attitudes and actively stretch and develop the learning, with frequent participation in collaborative experiences. Children are actively encouraged to direct experiences	Positive learning dispositions and attitudes developed and extended	I can learn in a number of places, in a number of ways with adults who challenge and support my creative thinking

Source: Adapted from Claxton and Carr's (2004) typology of environments

Reflection point 3.2

Consider two different early years environments that you might come across as an early years practitioner. These might be settings you have worked in, or attended for placement. They might be settings that you take your own children to, or have attended yourself. Now look at the list you created in Chapter 1 about what makes quality practice 'quality'. What might some of the obstacles or challenges be that you face in creating a quality environment, and how might you overcome them to enable 'quality provision'?

Creating the potentiating learning environment

So how might we go about creating a potentiating environment, or transforming an existing environment into one, with the quality outcomes that it brings? Claxton and Carr's (2004) descriptions tell us what it might look like, and what opportunities might exist within it, but in this section we will consider some of the practical steps that early years practitioners can take to develop these environments.

A high-quality learning environment should not simply invite children, but should by its very nature be a provocation to learn, drawing children in so that they are encouraged to express their dispositions towards learning, their attitudes and their preferences, and allowing them to select those experiences and activities that are meaningful to them and that foster relationships and communication (Curtis & Carter, 2003). In order to develop such environments, practitioners need to consider carefully how best to explore and build on the interests and experiences of the children. Children's curiosity is invoked by the physical world around them and how it works, so attempting to create a learning environment that replicates the experiences and opportunities outside the setting, and which provokes a comparable sense of wonder, curiosity and excitement is a useful approach.

We can do this by:

1   Mirroring the way children learn holistically
2   Helping children to make connections and have a sense of belonging
3   Being flexible and encouraging independent access to materials by children
4   Providing time and space to explore, create and hypothesize
5   Enabling children to learn both inside and outside the classroom

We will now look at each of these in turn.

Holistic learning

The natural world (if we take this as our starting point) is not organized according to the subjects of the curriculum or the EYFS! Young children do not perceive their learning in terms of subjects: they learn holistically and their learning will encompass a range of subjects, activities and interactions, wherever they happen to be. It is very hard to separate elements of literacy from numeracy, understanding the world and personal and social development, when children are actively engaged in an activity such as planting seed potatoes. It is not even clear whether the indoors/outdoors distinction holds for many such activities.

There are advantages to organizing environments in a defined arrangement around the areas of learning: it may have the benefit of making discrete aspects of learning visible, so we might have a maths table, a writing table, a small world play area for example, but this is probably more for the benefit of the adults than the children. But for a quality learning environment that mirrors experiences beyond the setting, it is often much more helpful to decide on a set of key learning experiences to be offered rather than learning outcomes to be addressed, and then identify how these possibilities might be addressed across the whole environment, linked to whatever curriculum is then in place. This can specifically be reflected in the planning: learning outcomes can be matched to the key resources, routines and experiences on offer to guide staff and reassure parents and Ofsted inspectors that quality learning opportunities are offered everywhere and at all times. The 'home corner', therefore, can be used to offer a whole range of learning opportunities as Figure 3.2 shows.

Literacy: signs, shopping lists, recipes ....   Numeracy: which size of pan do I need?   Decorations reflect children's homes and communites

Developing imagination and communication through role play   Opportunities to socialise and talk informally

Figure 3.2 The home corner

All areas of the curriculum can be accessed in the home corner in a holistic, meaningful and safe way. Children can be encouraged to write out shopping lists, estimate the size of pans or the number of slices of pizza they will need to share with the children playing alongside them, and to spend time socializing, story-making and role-playing.

Young infants begin to learn from their immediate surroundings and daily experiences using all of their senses. They touch, taste, smell, observe and move in the world around them to make sense out of it. Even before infants can crawl, adults should provide a variety of sensory experiences and encourage movement and playfulness. Environments should engage the infants' large and small muscles, captivate their senses and activate their curiosity. The sense of well-being and security conveyed by adults in an appropriate environment helps create a readiness for other experiences. Mobile infants are active, independent and curious. They are increasingly persistent and purposeful in doing things, and they need many opportunities to practise new skills and explore the environment within safe boundaries.

Toddlers are developing new language skills, physical control and awareness of themselves and others each day. They enjoy participation in planned and group activities, but they are not yet ready to sit still or work in a group for very long. Adults can support toddlers' learning in all areas by maintaining an environment that is secure and dependable, but flexible enough to provide opportunities for them to extend their skills, understanding and judgement in individual ways.

Connecting and belonging

Claxton and Carr (2004) suggest that creating a potentiating learning environment, which fosters positive learning dispositions, requires frequent and continuing participation in shared activities, including those initiated by the children themselves. This means organizing the learning environment to encourage social experiences, where children work, talk and play together with other children, and with adults, to negotiate and connect their learning to their experiences, interests and dispositions. With that in mind, adults need to reflect on the way in which the setting is organized and attempt to maximize opportunities for sharing and talking. This means thinking about the number of tables and chairs, physical barriers and perhaps avoiding strict designated areas that might prevent such fluid, negotiated learning from occurring. Does learning always take place on or around a table? The answer to that is clearly no!

Another prerequisite for this connected learning is for children to feel safe and secure in the learning environment: they belong. Building strong connections amongst the children, families and their communities, as well as within the setting itself, helps children to feel a real sense of belonging. Having places where children and parents can feel comfortable and encounter meaningful, recognizable experiences that, in part, mirror their home lives can add considerably to the children's well-being and dispositions to learn.

We have talked about the importance of the role of the 'key person' else-where (especially in Chapters 1 and 2). It is vital that roles are organized within the setting to foster a sense of belonging and security for young children and the key person is crucial here as they are best placed to be attentive to their needs, to understand what out-of-school experiences might be relevant, and to monitor progress and scaffold new experiences. Adults often underestimate the impor-tance of their role in children's learning and forget that they are not simply organ-izers or guides, but partners in children's making of meanings and it is through our interactions that we help to shape their dispositions and attitudes to learning.

Flexible spaces for independent learning

While children do need to feel safe and secure, constantly changing the organi-zation of the learning environment is not to be encouraged; it is important that the space can respond to their ever-changing curiosity, interests and needs. This means that even though practitioners may have put a great deal of time into developing a learning area, they have to be willing to see it used in unexpected ways, respond to children breaking the boundaries they may have had in mind (the vegetables from the home corner might be appropriated to be 'planted' in a sand tray or mud kitchen, or the whole area might be reorganized to become part of a café), and change and develop it accordingly.

Children can make connections in their learning that adults may never have considered and sometimes these need to be carefully managed by adults: while the disappearance of carrots into the outdoor mud kitchen may be a minor concern, the appearance of large amounts of mud in every cooking pot is more serious and may involve a good deal of cleaning up. However, more often than not, the connec-tions children make are valid, and indeed creative, and the challenge for teachers is to be attentive, to tune into them and try and keep up with the children's thinking!

At the same time, there are some boundaries that need to be established but this can be done in a way that makes sense to the children and reinforces positive social behaviours: snacks are eaten sitting down, bicycles and muddy boots stay outdoors, and other children's space and belongings are respected. We, as adults, are often the ones that need to remember to be flexible: the 'holistic' learning dis-cussed above needs also to allow children to use and take over spaces, and to transfer resources, skills and activities across boundaries we set up in the class-room. In order for children to be able to pursue their ideas and learning interests with as much autonomy as possible, the resources need to be organized in such a way as to promote children's independence and resilience. This combination of flexibility and attentiveness, argue Dweck, Claxton and Carr (2000, 2004), and others, will support children gain mastery over their learning, allow them to make mistakes in their experimentation and build resilience, so fostering intrinsic moti-vation and higher levels of engagement.

Time to explore, create and hypothesize

Having talked about 'space', now we turn to 'time'! How time is organized in early years environments can significantly affect the learning that goes on. Children should be given the time, as well as the space, to follow their interests through to a meaningful conclusion; this may mean that they are able to persist with activities, return to projects and save their work—whether this is a piece of writing, a drawing, the product of a craft activity or a work on a computer. All of these practical aspects, and the conversations around them, contribute to the sustained learning that characterizes a high-quality learning environment.

What this may mean in practice is that flexibility depends on routines being established. This may seem counterintuitive, but it allows children to become involved in a degree of forward planning, which practitioners can scaffold. How long will this take? Do I have enough time for this, or should I come back to this tomorrow? Does this painting need to dry before I take it home? Where routines are constantly changing, children may be interrupted in their activities: they may be unable to plan, or persist, become frustrated in their efforts and lose interest in their learning. This has an emotional aspect as well: the organization of time can impact on well-being, involvement and positive dispositions for learning: children that are rushed between activities and spaces, and do not have sufficient time to revel in and enjoy their learning, will not feel satisfaction and this can impact their behaviour in the setting. Seeing an activity through to its conclusion is important and teachers need to provide time, as well as encouragement, for children to do this.

The outside learning environment

Time spent learning outside may well be more valuable for some children than time learning indoors, as it will suit their preferred way of learning. In Scandinavia much of the learning takes place outdoors, and it is recognized as a very important learning environment. Learning outcomes in countries like Finland are high, and indicate quality early years provision, yet most of the time children are outside learning and playing until they are 6 or 7 years old (Organization for Economic Co-operation and Development , 2012). The first version of the EYFS (Department for Children, Schools and families, 2008) placed high importance on outdoor learning taking place regularly but this aspect has since been weakened in the current framework which requires only that 'providers must provide access to an outdoor play area or, if that is not possible, ensure that outdoor activities are planned and taken on a daily basis' (Department for Education, 2014, p. 24). We know that physical skills are developed outside, but so are social, cognitive and emotional skills and competences. Maude (2006) links play and movement, and suggests they are vital for a child's ability to participate in educational activities; furthermore, that children with a broader range of gross and fine motor skills have an educational advantage over children who are less proficient in those areas. In the same way, studies such as those by Sigmund, Sigmundova, and Ansari (2008), which showed that children in the equivalent of Year 1 in the Czech Republic had significantly lower levels of physical activity in school than in Sweden, have suggested it was affecting young children's abilities to concentrate and educational progress.

Despite this kind of evidence, the outdoor learning environment is often neglected, as it is often not perceived as a classroom, which often leads to impoverished provision and lack of attention to potential learning opportunities. This is an unhelpful perception as it fails to maximize the unique nature of the outdoor teaching and learning space, and does not take into account children's preferences, especially boys, for outdoor learning (Bilton, 2010; Fisher, 2010). The outside learning environment should be seen as an extension of the indoor learning environment and all of the prime and specific areas of learning and development of the EYFS curriculum can be made available outside. That said, what they look like outside may be very different from the way they look inside, as being outdoors offers opportunities for doing things in different ways and on different scales than when indoors (Table 3.2).

Even in the most challenging spaces, careful rotation of high-quality resources can promote excellent learning activities for young children. The smallest of outdoor spaces can be transformed with the use of resource boxes and careful attention to children's interests.

Table 3.2: Indoor and Outdoor Activities Compared

Indoor activities	Links to the EYFS	Outdoor activities
Sewing activities on binca with darning needles and beads, scraps of material	Physical development Expressive arts and design	Ribbon weaving across railings of fences
Unit blocks	Mathematical development	Hollow blocks requiring greater space
Mixing powder paints and representation. Working with Paint brushes, paper, jugs, etc.	Physical development Literacy expressive Arts and design Understanding the world	Mud and water: mixing and representation. Using sticks, watering cans, etc.
Home corner with domestic play resources	PSED Physical development Understanding the world Expressive arts and design	Den making with a range of open-ended materials or a mud kitchen

Reflection point 3.3

Put yourself in the shoes of a young child in a setting and consider what the learning environment looks like from their perspective? Use the statements below, from the perspective of the child, to reflect on your placement or setting.

1. I can see who I am and what I like to do at home and at school.
2. There are cosy spaces where my carer can sit and speak to me or my key worker.
3. There are wondrous and magical things to do here.
4. I can make representations from what I understand or imagine here.
5. I can feel powerful and be physically active here.
6. I can learn to see things from different perspectives here.
7. I feel safe here to make mistakes and learn from them here.
8. I am a confident and capable learner here! (Adapted from Curtis & Carter, 2003)

Challenges facing the development of a quality learning environment

Quality learning environments spring from the principles outlined earlier in the chapter. Different stakeholders may very well have different views and expectations of what the learning environment should look like, and these views may well be sufficiently powerful to drive the environment in a particular direction. Here are just a few of the potential influences on practice.

External forces

Although the EYFS in England makes suggestions as to what learning might look like in the enabling environments element of the Development Matters (Department for Education 2014; Early Education, 2012), the suggestions are not prescriptive. Influences may arise from the EYFS emphasis on school readiness and the Ofsted inspection regime with its focus on learning and development in literacy and numeracy. Ofsted (2014) state that early years providers must ensure a good level of development and school readiness for children. However, while acknowledging the complexity of judging quality environments, it offers little advice on what that might look like in practice. This could lead to an environment where more formal literacy and numeracy teaching is favoured in place of a more holistic approach in a mistaken attempt to get children ready for school. These influences, then, may cause tension between our vision and values and the need to meet external targets and standards-driven outcomes.

Top-down pressure

Similarly, the phonics assessment in Year 1 may influence provision in reception classes; an increased emphasis on phonics may result in pressure to adopt a more formal pedagogy that requires tabletop work with less time spent on more holistic learning methods and playful learning, with more experiential resources and activities being replaced with more overtly formal teaching tools (Goouch & Lambirth, 2011). This top-down view of learning, where children need to conform to the rigid beliefs of a stage-driven learning process, can result in an arid environment in which play, exploration, risk-taking and a growth mindset are not valued (Dweck, 2000).

Adults' understanding of the value of playful learning

While play is often highly valued in preschools, it is less often the case in the primary school where it is viewed more as being outside of pedagogy and occurs less frequently. We do not always give time or space for it in the day. Routines such as 'choosing time' or 'golden time' really go against the principles outlined above. McInnes, Howard, Miles and Crowley (2011, p.121) argue that there is often a 'mismatch' between teachers' views of the value of play and how they facilitate the playful learning in the classroom, with resultant affect on the physical environment.

The impact of assessment

Although the EYFS Statutory Framework suggests play as an important feature of the curriculum, an increasingly more formal approach during the reception year to prepare the children for Year 1 is advocated (Department for Education, 2014; Early Education, 2014). We need to be especially careful here as we move towards a new regime of assessment for young children in reception classes. While the playful characteristics of learning are integral, there is undeniably a tension with the focus on literacy and mathematics in the specific areas of learning (Nutbrown, 2015). The baseline tests in force from September 2016 may similarly affect the way the learning environment is constructed as the testing moves earlier and earlier for young children, and practitioners may feel compelled to rethink pedagogy and reorganize provision in response to the results of the baseline tests.

> ### Reflection point 3.4
>
> With an ever-increasing drive to ensure 'school readiness' and to assess children's learning, practitioners may be unwittingly influenced to create a more 'formal' learning environment. How the curriculum becomes enacted within a particular environment is discussed further in Chapter 6.
>
> When you visit a local early years setting, where can you see influences of policy in the design of the environment? How does this represent 'quality'?

References

Bilton, H. (2010). *Outdoor learning in the early years: Management and innovation.* (3rd ed.). Abingdon: David Fulton.

Bodrova, E., & Leong, D. (2005). Uniquely preschool: What research tells us about the ways young children learn. *Educational Leadership, 63*(1), 44–47.

Bowlby, J. (1953). *Child care and the growth of love.* Harmondsworth: Penguin.

Brownlee, J., & Berthelsen, D. (2006). Personal epistemology and relational pedagogy in early childhood teacher education programs. *Early Years, 26*(1), 17–29.

Ceppi, G., & Zini, M. (Eds.). (1998). *Children, spaces, relations: Metaproject for an environment for young children.* Milan: Domus Academy Research Centre.

Chawla-Duggan, R. (2011). Working with practitioners' perspectives: Supporting father involvement in family services in England. *Early Years: An International Journal of Research and Development, 31*(2), 149–161.

Clarke, A., & Moss, P. (2001). *Listening to young children: The mosaic approach.* London: National Children's Bureau.

Claxton, G., & Carr, M. (2004). A framework for teaching learning: learning dispositions. *Early Years International Journal of Research and Development, 24*(1), 87–97.

Claxton, G. (2006). *Building learning power* (2nd ed.). Bristol: The Learning Organisation.

Curtis, D., & Carter, M. (2003). *Designs for living and learning.* St. Paul, MN: Red Leaf.

Department for Children, Schools and Families. (2008). *Statutory framework for the early years foundation stage.* London: DCSF.

Department for Education. (2014). *Statutory framework for the early years foundation stage.* London: DfE.

Dweck, C. (2000*). Self-theories: Their role in motivation, personality, and development.* New York and London: Taylor & Francis/Psychology Press.

Early Education. (2012). *Development matters in the early years foundation stage* (EYFS). British Association for Early Childhood Education/Department for Education.

Edwards, C., Gandini, L., & Forman, G. (1998). *The hundred languages of children* (2nd ed.). Westport: Ablex.

Fisher, J. (2010). *Starting from the child* (3rd ed.). Maidenhead: Open University Press.

Goouch, K., & Lambirth, A. (2011). *Teaching early reading and phonics: Creative approaches to early literacy.* London: Sage.

Guha, M. (1987). Play in school. In G. Blenkin & A. Kelly (Eds.), *Early childhood education.* (pp. 56–73). London: Paul Chapman.

Harms, T., Clifford, R., & Cryer, D. (2005). *Early childhood environment rating scale - revised edition.* New York, NY: Teachers College Press.

Isenberg, J., & Quisenberry, N. (2002). Play: Essential for all children. *Childhood Education, 79*(1), 33–39.

Jarman, E. (2007). *Communication friendly spaces.* London: Basic Skills Agency.

Laevers, F. (1994). *The Leuven involvement scale for young children LIS-YC, manual and videotape* (Experiential Education Series No. 1). Leuven, Belgium: University of Leuven.

Maccoby, E. (2007). Historical overview of socialization research and theory. In J. E. Grusec & P. D. Hastings (Eds.), *Handbook of socialization theory and research* (pp. 13–41). New York and London: Guilford Press.

Malaguzzi, L. (1993). For an education based on relationship. *Young Children, 49*(1), 9–12.

Maude, P. (2006). 'How do I do this better?' From movement development to physical literacy. In D. Whitebread (Ed.), *Teaching and learning in the early years* (2nd ed., pp. 211–228). London: Routledge.

McInnes, K., Howard, J., Miles, G., & Crowley K. (2011). Differences in practitioners' understanding of play and how this influences pedagogy and children's perceptions of play. *Early Years: An International Research Journal, 32*(2): 121–133.

Moyles, J. (2010). *The excellence of play.* Maidenhead: Open University Press.

Nutbrown, C. (2015) *We must scrap new baseline tests for primary school children.* Retrieved on June 22, 2015, from https://theconversation.com/we-must-scrap-new-baseline-tests-for-primary-school-children-36558

Organization for Economic Co-operation and Development. (2010). *Starting strong 11: Early childhood education and care.* Retrieved June 1, 2015, from http://www.oecd.org/edu/preschoolandschool/37519079.pdf

Organization for Economic Co-operation and Development. (2012). *PISA 2012 results in focus.* Retrieved June 1, 2015, from http://www.oecd.org/pisa/keyfindings/pisa-2012-results-overview.pdf

Piaget, J., & Inhelder, B. (1969). *The psychology of the child.* New York: Basic Books.

Robinson, M. (2008). *Child development 0–8: A journey through the early years.* Maidenhead: Open University Press.

Rogoff, B. (1990). *Apprentice in thinking: Cognitive development in a social context:* New York: Oxford University Press.

Rogoff, B. (2003). *The cultural nature of human development.* New York: Oxford University Press.

Sigmund, E., Sigmundova, D., & Ansari, W. (2008). Changes in physical activity in pre- schoolers and first grade children: Longitudinal study in the Czech Republic. *Child: Care, Health and Development, 35*(3), 376–382.

Smidt, S. (2006). *The developing child in the 21st century: A global perspective on child development.* London and New York: Routledge.

Sylva, K., Melhuish, E., Sammons, P., Siraj-Blatchford, I., & Taggart, B. (2004). *The Effective Provision of Pre-School Education (EPPE) Project: Final report.* A longitudinal study funded by the Department for Education and Skills DfES 1997–2004. London: DfES.

United Nations General Assembly. (1989). *Convention on the Rights of the Child,* 20 November 1989. UN Treaty Series, vol. 1577.

Vygotsky, L. (1978). *Mind in society: The development of higher psychological processes.* Cambridge, MA: Harvard University Press.

Whitebread, D. (2012). *Developmental psychology and early childhood education.* London: Sage.

Williams, L., & De Gaetano, Y. (1985). *A multicultural, bilingual approach to teaching young children.* New York: Addison-Wesley.

4   Developing quality relationships

Julie Beams

This chapter invites you to explore notions of what quality relationships might entail within an early years setting. To do this, you will be encouraged to first reflect on who you might be brokering professional relationships with, for what purpose, and the impact they will have on the potential to accomplish in children's care and learning.

To start these reflections you might find it useful to think about who holds the responsibility for forming such relationships; practitioners, parents or someone else—and do both have equal responsibility or should one party lead the process? Beyond but related to this, who holds responsibility for maintaining such relationships once they are formed? These will form two key areas of enquiry within this chapter as you consider the skills, dispositions and attitudes that are needed to ensure those effective relationships. The fact that you are reading this chapter suggests that you feel you have some part to play in each of these processes, and as you move through the chapter you will be alerted to different avenues of support you might look to in order to ensure your own practice fosters positive relationships within the early years setting.

In your initial reflections in Chapter 1, you possibly made reference to relational aspects of practice as being important in delivering quality provision. Here we take the view that relationships in a variety of forms are a vital plank in the construction of quality provision and the support systems that can help to develop these.

What are quality relationships?

Those relationships, which are treasured or valued by those who enter into them, might be one indicator that they are of quality. It is likely that to feel valued, those engaged in any form of relationship will also need to feel respected by one another, and in a professional capacity this is primarily based on respect for the commitments, knowledge and skills that the other person brings to the relationship. Additional descriptors might include terms such as 'supportive' or 'caring'. We shall explore towards the end of the chapter how this is important within multi-agency working, but the central part of the chapter will look at individual relationships within the setting itself.

Fostering a strong emotional climate, for both adults and children alike, is a principal contributory factor in creating a quality environment. A mutually enhancing environment can harness and combine the skills of all who are party to that environment. Therefore, it is important to focus on ensuring that adults in a setting engage in quality relationships which can have a direct and positive impact on the learning experience offered to children within that setting.

Having looked briefly at some of the overarching principles that underpin quality relationships generally, we shall now consider more deeply some of the key individual and specific relationships that you may be part of, or lead, within early years practice.

Practitioners with children

The need for adults to develop quality relationships with the children in their care is self-evident. The seminal work of Goldschmeid and Jackson (2003), Elfer and Dearnley (2007) and Elfer, Goldschmied, and Selleck (2012) provide us with a range of evidence and explanations of how positive relationships between adults and children positively support children's learning and development. Further embedded as an underpinning principle within recent early years policy, most notably *Birth to three matters* (Department for Education and Skills, 2002) and subsequent Early Years Foundation Stage (EYFS) frameworks (Department for Children, Schools and Families, 2008; Department for Education, 2012, 2014), further reinforces the widely accepted notion that the adult–child relationship is key and central to quality provision.

The EYFS suggests that it is the role of the 'key person' to ensure that children feel welcome, enjoy a sense of belonging and have a close relationship that sustains them while they are apart from their key carer(s). While this point cannot be overstated, it is one that is possibly undervalued, not least by society more generally certainly, as there is little recognition of the emotional labour that the undertaking of a key person role carries. The emotional aspect of early years practice is covered in more detail in other chapters in this book.

Children with children

Quality relationships between children will undoubtedly be a vital component in the life and provision of any setting. Taking a sociocultural approach to children's experiences, care and learning, Rogoff (1990) and Vygotsky (1978) remind us of the critical role that interactions with others play in children's developing knowledge of their world, themselves and one another. Likewise, Dunn (1988, 2004) gives rise to our increased knowledge of the importance of friendships in supporting young children's social and emotional development, as well as its central role in fostering the ability to see others' perspectives: a key life skill.

This has implications for both planning and the creation of the learning environment, which are covered in Chapter 3. You might like to consider here, therefore, what the implications of 'not' providing such a climate for children might be before you move on to the following reflection point.

Reflection point 4.1

Are children 'beings' or 'becomings'? As Brownlee and Berthelsen (2006) note, our world view has a significant impact on the way we provide a potentiating environment for children and enable them to have a voice and hence 'quality' provision. (See Chapter 3 for a further discussion on environments).

Children with children across the setting: time for siblings to be together

Elfer et al. (2012) and Manning-Morton and Thorp (2015) note the importance for children, particularly the youngest children, to have time for some kind of familial contact with siblings during the day, including time spent within their early years provision. Their view is that younger children can be settled and reassured by the presence of their older sibling in their room, with times for children to mix through the setting where feasible or while mixing together in outdoor play sessions. Even those who appear settled and secure within a setting can still be negatively affected by raised cortisol within their brain simply due to the 'stress' of the fact that their day-care setting is a secondary place and not home. Gerhardt (2004) explores the damaging effects of cortisol, although she reminds us that we have no sure way of knowing just from observing a child whether their cortisol is raised—but we are able to make some informed guesses as to their mental and emotional state at various times of the day. An alert and responsive key person, who has a strong and effective relationship with their key child or children, will be able to do this and will be able to act to try and reduce any stress in children that they perceive. This again, then, highlights the critical key person role, but further still raises the issue of the organizational day and how time and space are managed to give children opportunities to see siblings and friends in informal spaces.

Vignette: Michelle

Michelle had just started in the school's nursery class, and Dawn, her sister, had moved in reception in the same school. Michelle took some time to settle. She did not explore very many areas that the inside and outside provision offered, tended to 'flit' anxiously and would not be parted from her 'blankie'. Towards the end of the settling-in period, staff from the nursery and reception classes met at a foundation stage unit to discuss the process overall and individual children in particular. The nursery staff raised their concerns about Michelle, given that they had not experienced anything like this with Dawn when she joined the setting.

It was decided that opening up the unit, so children could move more freely between the nursery base and the reception classroom areas, might be a useful thing to do from a good practice point of view. However, it was also hoped that perhaps if Dawn could spend a bit more time with Michelle, she could help her to explore more freely and with less anxiety.

As a result of this change of organization, Michelle became much braver in the setting. She knew that there were times when she could see Dawn and as a result relaxed more into her play. As time went on, 'blankie', the transitional object, reduced in significance until, by the end of the year, it was permanently in the cloakroom—but Michelle knew she could visit it if she ever felt she needed to. Dawn had supported this key transition for her sister, and the opportunity for children to flow more freely through the foundation unit seemed to benefit many children who were able to form friendships and support each other in their learning and play.

The above scenario indicates how, with some good communication between practitioners based in different parts of a school setting, children can have opportunities to make the setting 'more like home', and with the additional development, the transitional object for Michelle was able to become less of a necessary focus for her, thus allowing her to access a wider range of opportunities offered to her within the environment.

Practitioners and parents

Reflection point 4.2

'Parents are most frequently the child's first and most enduring educator.' How many times have you heard this statement before? How far do you really subscribe to this viewpoint? And if you genuinely do, what implications does that have for developing quality relationships that work for the benefit of all involved and in particular for the child's care, learning and well-being?

The importance of cultivating respectful, informative and caring relationships between parent and practitioner cannot be overstated. A range of key literature (Fitzgerald, 2004; Whalley, 2008; Wheeler & Connor, 2009) and government documents and frameworks (for example, Department for Education, 2014; Department for Education and Skills, 2002, 2006) recognize this, along with highlighting some key ways in which these positive relationships can be brokered and maintained. Genuine interest, being welcoming, open and honest, and making time for informal dialogue while maintaining professional boundaries are all key elements in making appropriate relationships with parents work. And in all cases, some broader understanding and appreciation of a child's family circumstances are of benefit to all, and particularly so where there are additional vulnerabilities, disadvantages or challenges present within a child's life.

In order for you to develop the quality you seek within your relationships with parents, you first need to consider your personal values and beliefs. How do you see parents? For example as:

- experts on their own children
- always significant and effective teachers of their own children
- skilled in ways that complement those of practitioners
- different, but with equal strengths and equivalent expertise
- able to make informed observations and impart information to practitioners
- inherently involved in the lives and well-being of their children
- able to contribute to and be central in decision making
- responsible and able to share accountability with practitioners

The above represent some challenging reflection points, and are worth while spending time considering, both as an individual and as a team. As professionals, it is not always a straightforward matter of developing equal partnerships with the whole range of parents that you might encounter in a setting. Some parents might not appear ready, willing or able to engage. However, given that the earlier part of this chapter recognized that these relationships are worth striving for, then it is also clear that professional actions need to match those beliefs, and it is vital that early years professionals reflect on how they ensure those values are enacted in their practice. Continual reflection will, therefore, ultimately help that journey towards quality.

Malaguzzi, writing in the context of the Reggio Emilia approach notes that:

> Family participation requires many things, but most of all it demands ... a multitude of adjustments. [Practitioners] must possess a habit of questioning their certainties, a growth of sensitivity, awareness and availability [in order to gain] continually updated knowledge of children, an

enriched evaluation of parental roles, and skills to talk, listen and learn from parents. (Malaguzzi, 1998, p. 63)

Malaguzzi here notes the importance of the reflective practitioner: one who reflects both on both beliefs and actions in the quest to ensure that relationships are strong and nurturing for all concerned.

Reflection point 4.3

The Department for Education (DfE 2014) Code of Practice notes the following:

- Recognition that parents play a 'critical role'.
- All parents of children with Special Educational Needs (SEN) should be treated as 'partners'.
- Ensure that parents understand procedures, are aware of how to access support in preparing their contributions, and are given documents to be discussed well before meetings.
- Respect the validity of differing perspectives and seek constructive ways of reconciling different viewpoints.
- Respect the differing needs parents themselves may have, such as a disability, or communication and linguistic barriers.
- Recognize the need for flexibility in the timing and structure of meetings.
- These principles cut across the needs of Special Educational Needs and Disabilities (SEND) and other children and their parents, and are worth reflecting on in terms of general partnerships with parents in the setting.

How do the above ideas relate to your view of quality and your practice, and how do these relate to the notes you made in Chapter 1 about what constitutes 'quality early years provision'? You might think about:

- What skills and qualities should practitioners possess and develop in order to nurture these kinds of relationships with parents?
- What practical considerations might be needed for the organization of your time or the scheduling of the setting's sessions?

Practitioners with each other

While the notion of quality is a slippery concept, as Dahlberg, Moss, and Pence (2007) note, it needs to be acknowledged that some objective 'markers' should be considered, as indeed Office for Standards in Education, Children's Services and Skills (Ofsted) will do during the inspection process. Some key pointers are those of noting the quality of teamwork within settings. For quality practice, it is vital that practitioners in teams work harmoniously, sharing similar values, goals and beliefs. The most effective teams are those motivated by a shared vision, and have leadership that both inspires and enables good practice. However, this does not necessarily signify what Edgington, 2004 calls a 'cosy' team. These 'cosy' teams are not forward- or outward-looking. While some introspection is absolutely necessary when teams and individuals reflect on their practice, it is mainly through seeking support from outside of the team that the nudge for change occurs—through visits to other settings or professional dialogue with colleagues in other settings, through training and Continuing Professional Development (CPD) opportunities, or through keeping abreast of current research messages through reading journals or professional magazines.

Practitioners, therefore, need to adopt what Edgington terms a 'rigorously challenging' stance when working in teams. This means questioning practice, while maintaining a healthy respect for colleagues' knowledge, skills and expertise. It means reflecting and problematizing the 'taken-for-granted' aspects of practice: these might not always be the most effective way of doing something, even though they may have been once. Even those relatively new to the field of early years will no doubt have already begun to pick up on the myriad of changes that have taken place in recent years. The suggestion, therefore, that what was 'good' and 'effective' before might not necessarily be what is needed or expected now.

Reflection, therefore, is a critical component in striving towards a notion of quality provision and quality improvement. It helps to keep children at the forefront of pedagogical practice through what Dewey terms the 'active, persistent and careful consideration of belief or supposed form of knowledge' (1910, p. 6). Furthermore, as Senge (2006) notes, critically reflective practitioners typically have increased morale, commitment to clients, and openness to multiple perspectives and creative, innovative solutions to issues—all of which are vital if early years practitioners are to remain flexible and responsive to the changing demands placed on the sector.

Reflection point 4.4

Consider the following scenarios and how they might give pause for reflection.

Setting X has always offered a sit-down snack time with all the children without considering why it does this or what alternatives there might be. A change in policy which admits more 2-year-old children now means that snack times are fraught, irritable and unhappy for children and practitioners as the very young children struggle to acclimatize to the routine and expectations.

A new early years teacher in Setting Y has noticed that 'creative' activities are really just craft sessions, where a limited number of resources are set out and a finished product is shown to the children as a model and children are expected to reproduce this. Other staff in Setting Y are well established there, and say the parents like to see children's art work done in this way.

Setting Z's policy is that if two children are seen fighting, they are separated by staff and spoken to. They have a five-minute time out and then staff tell them they have to say 'sorry' to each other before being allowed to go and play again.

- What values are taken for granted in these settings/scenarios?
- How might they be viewed by the different participants?
- How might notions of quality practice be debated and explored by teams here?

Leaders have a pivotal role to play in enabling practitioners to work together although, of course, a leader can only be a leader if there are followers! Practitioners need to be motivated to work together well, under the direction of the leader who should be setting the ethos, the vision, the trust and suitable communication channels for the team as a whole to be effective, as well as practitioners individually within it to work well. Hence, strong but sensitive leaders have a significant role to play in facilitating quality relationships within the setting and it is to this set of concepts that the next section turns.

Practitioners with their leaders and managers

The developing growth of literature about the qualities of leaders and managers in the early years field is a relatively recent phenomenon (see, for example, Lindon & Lindon, 2011; Moyles, 2006; Muijs, Aubrey, Harris, & Briggs, 2004; Rodd, 2006; Siraj-Blatchford & Hallett, 2014). While debate and discussion abounds regarding traits of leaders and management styles and approaches in certain situations, what is clear is that there are some important factors when it comes to the abilities of leaders to be effective. You will also have your own ideas of what constitutes effective leadership, perhaps based on your own experiences of being led yourself. Considering your own experiences alongside the literature noted above, it is likely that you will have a list including terms such as 'respectful, visionary, empathetic, approachable, a good listener and communicator', and so on.

Such 'leaderful qualities' are worth reflecting on as pointers towards effective quality practice. However, it must be noted that regardless of the qualities you identified, these qualities might not solely rest with those who have a designated leadership responsibility—in the words of respondents in the study by Rodd, 'leadership can be undertaken for an hour, a day or a year' (2006, p. 13) and they can be 'room supervisors or policy makers but whoever they are they are usually committed to moving practice on' (Rodd, 2006, p. 42). Nutbrown also notes that they should be people who have a clear and principled approach to the education and care of young children based on knowledge of theory and child development (Department for Education, 2012). However, these traits are worth reflecting on, given that a quest for quality clearly extends beyond the boundaries of what happens in the room that the children are in each day and out to the complex web of relationships that surround this.

Leadership has a significant impact on the quality of provision—it has an impact on the quality of the practitioners, on the imagination and scope of the environment, on the ethos of the setting and its aspirations to continually reflect on quality. A leader's words, actions and deployment of a multiplicity of interaction styles can significantly impact on the behaviour of others and how they respond in a team. They can impact as they work towards a common goal, make changes, build new mindsets and new ways of working (Rodd, 2006). The leader, therefore, is most likely to be at the centre of this web of relationships—influencing those relationships already discussed in this chapter and those still to come.

It is through this, therefore, that settings become transformed, and develop further along their journey to quality provision overall. If practitioners can come to trust and rely on leaders who are focused on improving quality while maintaining supportive and 'resonant' relationships (Goleman, Boyzatis, & McKee, 2002), they will feel supported, motivated and inspired in their work. Again, the ultimate beneficiaries are children; however, a spiral of positivity and purpose in all participants in the web of relationships begins to emerge from practice.

Practitioners, leaders and governing body, committee or advisory board

The symbiotic relationship between practitioners, leaders and their governing body (many of whom will also be parents) is one that echoes that of key worker and child, and leader and practitioner, with a focus on care, learning, challenge and support. The role of a setting's committee members, governing body or advisory board who share in the responsibility for leadership and who equally have some key input into and impact on the quality of a setting, and by implication, the relationships developed within it will, therefore, be considered here.

According to the website of the National Governors Association, for quality relationships to develop between them, the governing body needs to exercise the following attributes:

- the right people round the table
- understanding the role and responsibilities
- good chairing
- professional clerking

- good relationships based on trust
- knowing the school—the data, the staff, the parents, the children, the community
- committed to asking challenging questions
- confident to have courageous conversations in the interests of the children and young people

While undoubtedly the first few points are crucial here to the effectiveness of the smooth running of meetings in particular, it is the latter points that are argued here as having the greatest impact on relationships and ultimately on the quality enhancement of a setting. Clearly, both have parallels and resonance with the skills of a good leader.

Ofsted (2011), in their report into effective school governance noted the following key characteristics:

> Positive relationships between governors and school leaders are based on trust, openness and transparency. Effective governing bodies systematically monitor their school's progress towards meeting agreed development targets. Information about what is going well and why, and what is not going well and why, is shared. Governors consistently ask for more information, explanation or clarification. This makes a strong contribution to robust planning for improvement. Effective governing bodies are driven by a core of key governors such as the chair and chairs of committees. They see themselves as part of a team and build strong relationships with the head teacher, senior leaders and other governors . . . School leaders and governors behave with integrity and are mutually supportive. School leaders recognise that governors provide them with a different perspective, which contributes to strengthening leadership. The questions they ask challenge assumptions and support effective decision-making.

While the report from which this is taken is school-focused, the principles of strong and effective governance hold true for the range of settings that early years practitioners may find themselves in. Ofsted's inspection regime is increasingly scrutinizing the work of the governors, their relationships with the leader and the staff team, its knowledge of the setting it serves and the impact its work has. It is, therefore, imperative that governance is held as an important part of the web of relationships that develop and enhance quality provision for children.

Practitioners, leaders and wider support staff

Ideas of care, education, challenge and support arise again in discussion of the role of wider support personnel—local authority advisers, peripatetic personnel for children with additional needs, other agencies either co-located within or working in partnership with Children's Centres and their broader community remit. It is worth while reiterating that the outward-looking early years team should relish the opportunity to receive and share ideas and engage in dialogue with other professionals to enhance learning and provision, and to see this as a valuable source of CPD. The challenges of working in multidisciplinary and multi-agency teams (often co-located within the same building as in the case of many Children's Centres, but managed by different organizations and with different targets, vocabulary and professional processes) cannot be underestimated. However, the development of equal and active partnerships between the setting and wider support mechanisms can be a significantly positive relationship, if approached in a spirit of enquiry and seen as an opportunity to learn, develop and reflect on strengths and provide an impetus for change where needed.

While this chapter has so far presented the view that these ideas are important in the consideration of how we promote and maintain the complex web of quality relationships with the various stakeholders, the challenge and an intermediate reflection point here is this: how you perceive these notions and keep these ideas as a reflective focus of your work (individually and in your varied relationships within your settings, and in the early years sector in general) in order to keep ideas about quality provision and services to the forefront of what you do?

To ensure CPD, which allows you to develop not only your own practice but also that of the setting as a whole, requires a 'whole-setting' approach and yet each setting is made up of any number of very individual professionals. The second part of this chapter will, therefore, begin to explore in some more depth how this might be achieved or supported through the relationships that adults have with one another.

As mentioned earlier, in the same way that children's learning occurs through social interactions and experience, the same principles can be applied here for how leaders and managers refine their own skill sets. We will now particularly explore, therefore, two main issues as part of the current debate about quality support that is available to develop professional practice.

First, pedagogical practice; that is, what leaders and others within settings can do to enable practitioners individually and as part of a cohesive team to reflect on their practice and regularly update their knowledge base. The discussion includes a consideration of the opportunities and time they provide for CPD, supervision through coaching and mentoring as part of an overall vision for the support needed to move staff and teams to the position of quality provision and the formation and maintenance of reflective communities of practice that they envisage.

Second, the role and nature of the support that external personnel can provide, set against a backdrop of reducing budgets and shedding key support roles, and how this situation might be compensated by teams and leaders themselves within their own networks.

Support within settings

Pedagogical leadership is a way of leading learning—and in this case with the focus on leading learning towards a reflection on quality provision. It takes into account how learning can be promoted and sustained, through a complex web of decisions made about the strategies used that link the learner and the curriculum or subject matter under investigation, and underpinned by the values and knowledge of those involved. According to Siraj-Blatchford (2009), the best educators of young children use their knowledge about the interests and capabilities of the children in their care to provide what they believe is the most stimulating and effective range of learning experiences for them. So too, then, is this the case with effective pedagogical leaders: these are practitioners who play a critical role in supporting staff to maintain the interest, motivation and desire to reflect continuously on and improve their work with the children (Muijs et al., 2004; Sammons, Hillman, & Mortimore, 1999).

There is a range of drivers, however, which impact on pedagogical leadership, as illustrated below, and which indicate an interplay between Ofsted requirements and its specified indicators for good quality leadership practice and knowledge and theory. Strong leaders are able to absorb a range of frameworks and theories and apply the theoretical concepts in their own context and practice with the teams they lead (Figure 4.1).

Pedagogical leadership, therefore, is a learning-centred approach that recognizes the value of all involved in the school or centre being beholden to continue to learn and develop themselves—the team, therefore, become reflective 'learning professionals' (Guile & Lucas, 1999) and the leader of the setting (the 'lead learner') develops human capital by helping their setting to become learning communities of practice. What this does is add value—ultimately to the lives of the children but, in the process, to all of those involved in the joint venture of developing pedagogical understanding and thus to developing negotiated vision of quality.

The role of qualifications

The role of the critically reflective leader here, one who has a vision for improvement and inquiry and is driven ultimately by the need for children to gain the most from their experiences in their setting, is pivotal in helping staff to share in the venture. Whilst not exclusively the territory of graduate leaders—those with relevant degrees or Early Years Teacher Status (EYTS)—nevertheless, it needs to be recognized that the recent government push and investment in these areas is to be welcomed, encouraging leaders to demonstrate and model the highest possible commitment to early years practice in the teams they lead (Siraj-Blatchford & Hallett, 2014). Following on from the work of the Effective Provision of Pre-School Education (EPPE) project (Sylva, Melhuish, Sammons, Siraj-Blatchford, & Taggart, 2004), and echoed by government-commissioned reviews and reports

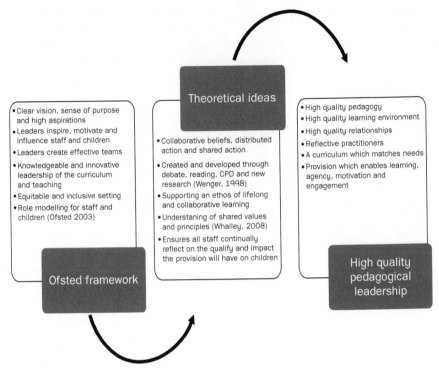

Figure 4.1 Characteristics of high-quality pedagogical leadership

published in 2013; Department for Education, 2012), it is known that a higher quality of provision is usually to be found in those settings where graduate leaders support less qualified staff, and settings that make most progress in their efforts to improve are generally those where there is both strong leadership and a higher proportion of graduate qualified staff.

This said, however, it is also understood that it is important for those graduates to see themselves as leaders of learning and to spend the vast proportion of their time within rooms modelling the good practice that their increased qualifications and expertise afford them. This is particularly important in settings where there are many children under 3 years old as, so far, early evaluations of the impact of graduate leaders and early years professionals (now known as early years teachers) note that by far the most positive effects have been recorded for children over 3 years old (Coleyshaw, Whitmarsh, Jopling, & Hadfield (2013)). In order to redress this balance and to continue to strive to raise the status of those working with children under 3 years old and supporting the youngest children in this very crucial time, it is important for graduate leaders and those with EYTS to lead practice more directly with children under 3 years old.

The Conservative Government's drive to place more 2-year-olds into settings and into school makes the case for our very youngest children's developmental needs to be recognized and supported ever more critical (Georgeson et al., 2014; Manning-Morton & Thorp, 2015). Our need, then, to have the knowledge and understanding of the unique young child, their family, their contexts and the way in which they access provision and experiences and to have time and space to reflect on what we see and how we use what we see well for the child is, therefore, possibly even more important than ever before within this current climate. Robust and relevant qualifications that support the practitioner to begin their journey in developing understanding of 'the winding developmental paths' (Manning-Morton & Thorp, 2015, p. 5) are, therefore, a key starting point in terms of quality support for practitioners. However, this is only one aspect of a complex picture that makes up quality practice.

CPD

CPD activity refers to a range of activities that practitioners might undertake, including professional training that is internal and external to the setting and professional support to develop job expertise and performance. These should develop professional growth, self-confidence and job satisfaction (Bubb & Earley, 2007), all of which should culminate in the idea of effective individuals working together in effective teams for the benefit of children and service users. The idea of CPD is generally accepted as an important one, as acknowledged by the Researching Effective Pedagogy in the Early Years (REPEY) report (Siraj-Blatchford, Sylva, Muttock, Gilden, & Bell, 2002). However, since this seminal report, there have been significant changes in the provision of CPD opportunities, which have changed the landscape of how CPD is procured and managed. Whereas once much of CPD on offer might have taken the form of in-service or short courses arranged and led by local authority personnel, this style of CPD has lost ground within the general reduction of local authority powers, personnel and budgets, and a new way forward for staff to continue to reflect and move forward in their learning has had to be forged.

From this perspective, then, the idea of in-house training, where a trainer comes to the whole staff team with a bespoke set of experiences and materials for that particular team and its current context, gains some resonance in terms of providing support for individuals and teams. While this does not give opportunities for staff members to look outside of their setting in the same way, what it does do is enable a 'fit' between the setting's needs and the direction of travel as a whole. It uses real-world problems—those that the setting experiences—and gives time for exploration of these issues through authentic discussion and, managed well, enables all involved to have a voice and perspective. Learning and moving forward, therefore, happens together in partnership, and firmer agreements can be made about how changes will be monitored, when further discussions will be shared and who will take a range of key responsibilities within this venture.

Formerly, the local authority early years advisory teacher (or similar) might have been an ideal person to assist. However, a reduction of personnel in many authorities means the onus may fall more on to the setting leader to become the most effective and knowledgeable that they can be: going on training courses, attending network events and cascading ideas back via team meetings and supervision.

The role of supervision

The idea of supervision as a means of providing professional support for practitioners is not a new thing, but is a feature that has taken longer to establish itself in many educational and care contexts. In social work, social care settings and case work areas, the idea of supervision, of being connected to one more 'expert' than oneself who can support apprenticeship into developing more expertise in a community of practice, has been one subscribed to for a much longer period of time. Supervision, therefore, should provide a positive space for compassion, enquiry, reflection and above all development. Done well, it should be both enabling and transforming.

Supervision came to wider prominence for early years settings when in the Tickell Review of the EYFS, it was stated:

> Supervision is primarily a tool to support the management of practice, and therefore a key part of staff support systems and a leader or manager's role. Where successful, it should provide practitioners with a route through which to raise any professional queries, to discuss career progression, to clarify roles, responsibilities and work tasks, to support performance management and to build their confidence in supporting children's development. (Department for Education, 2011, p. 46)

These sentiments have since become enshrined in later versions of the EYFS, which requires practitioners to be engaged in a cycle of supervision and appraisal—with the important point to make that they are different. While supervision may contain elements of discussion that might lend itself towards ideas that might be included in an annual appraisal (and Tickell notes here the words 'performance management'), it is primarily a tool that supports practitioners in steps and stages towards this (among other things)—much in the same way that, for example, ongoing observations of children, say in a reception class, might lead towards a final summative assessment as the Early Years Foundation Stage Profile (EYFSP) is built up over the year and then the overall judgements compiled in June each year.

What is worth highlighting here is the idea that supervision supports the development of quality practice for individuals—their personal and professional growth and self-development—and for that of the setting as a whole. It, therefore, contributes towards the idea of striving for quality within the setting, through professional, organized and reflective dialogic conversations—conversations which, for the practitioner, cover topics such as 'How am I?' 'How am I performing?' 'What roles am I managing?' 'What support do I need to do this most effectively?' 'What barriers am I experiencing in managing my roles?' 'What further challenges might I benefit from—now; in six month's time; in a year's time?' This again returns us to the idea of effective pedagogical leaders—those who do for their staff what a good practitioner does for their children: listening, containing fears and anxieties, scaffolding learning, offering positive encouragement and support, not shying away from finding ways of broaching issues about performance that need to be developed.

Supervision rests within the intersection of stakeholders' needs and the ways in which these needs are addressed. The stakeholders here are first and foremost the children, and their families; however, others do have a stake in the service we provide—the staff, managers, governors, advisory boards and committees, owners, partners and other agencies, and Ofsted as well. As the idea of supervision has become embedded in early years practice, so too does Ofsted inspect the effectiveness with which leaders and managers implement and work with a cycle of supervision. Ofsted (2012, p. 15) notes the following guidance within the grade descriptors for 'outstanding':

> High quality professional supervision is provided, based on consistent and sharply focused evaluations of the impact of staff's practice. An astute and targeted programme of professional development ensures practitioners are constantly improving their already first rate understanding and practice.

And for 'inadequate':

> Management and accountability arrangements are not clear or are not understood by providers and/or their managers. Practitioners are not encouraged to improve their knowledge or practice.

A 'good' grading takes into account 'effective systems' where 'practitioners are monitored and underperformance is tackled' and 'an effective and well established programme of professional development is helping practitioners to improve knowledge, understanding and practice'. This, therefore, helps leaders and managers in being accountable for those stakeholder needs, and ensuring that practitioners receive the support and development opportunities so that they can work well with colleagues and partners and deliver quality provision for children.

Key elements of supervision

The focus should be on critical reflection and analysis throughout, rooted within the practitioner's experience and working towards shared problem-solving of issues and a journey towards ways of moving forward in practice. A leader who has some experience of reflective cycles or frameworks for support or thinking (for example, those developed by Kolb, Gibbs, or Johns, which we will discuss shortly) should be able to lead the practitioner through their reflections, scaffolding as they do so, and leading the practitioner towards resolutions and action planning for their own development but primarily through listening and acknowledging the views and experiences of the practitioner. It may lead to the identification of or signposting towards further training, mentoring, counselling or coaching experiences as required—whatever presents itself as helpful to the practitioner and their needs and those that the setting has as goals are worked towards.

Kolb argues that any experience in life is one from which we can learn, reflect on what we have experienced, interpret and generate meanings and possibilities from these reflections and then make an active choice to act differently as a result (termed by Kolb as 'active experimentation'). Many of us pass through these stages possibly without theorizing them as such. While on the surface this appears to indicate a 'lone explorer' constructivist approach which might ignore the learning that can be achieved with others, nevertheless it is entirely possible for learners to be supported at each stage and step by others and an effective mentor (a leader, a more knowledgeable other, a peer) can support reflection, thinking and learning using these steps or stages as prompts.

Gibbs's cycle is another way for practitioners to examine their experiences from a range of possible angles, make sense of them and think through ways of changing and developing practice. Again, these stages could be reflected on alone; for example, through the use of a personal learning journal, or with a critical friend, be it a leader or peer. It is important that reflection is carried out within an emotionally and cognitively supportive environment where the practitioner trusts the person in order for reflection to be most effective and to have most impact on changing practice and moving it on.

Although coming from a background in nursing, Johns (2004) also provides a similar means of supporting us to think about our experiences through five 'cue questions':

- What is the description of the experience?
- Reflection (what was I trying to achieve? Why did I act the way I did?)
- Influencing factors (internal and external factors; sources of knowledge?)
- Evaluation (what other choices did I have? How might I have done better?)
- Learning (the synthesis between the feelings I have, the sense I have made of this situation and how I will 'know' in future?)

How frequently supervision sessions should take place is a matter for negotiation. Clearly, a transparent policy should be in place that highlights its value and

Vignette: The power of supervision as support for staff

Anna is responsible for the management of childcare in a children's centre on a very deprived estate on the edge of a large town. She is line-managed by the children's centre manager. The centre runs childcare provision as well as crèches for children whose parents are attending courses and groups in the Children's Centre. There was a concern about the way that the staff working with the children attending the crèche were planning learning activities, observing and recording progress and identifying next steps. It was felt that because the children only attended the crèche occasionally, there was less of a need for substantial adherence to EYFS principles. This was particularly noticeable for the sessional staff who worked in the crèche.

It was agreed in Anna's supervision that she would introduce monthly supervision and staff meetings as well as ensuring as far as possible that all sessional staff were able to attend these meetings. In addition, Anna worked more closely with the family workers to encourage better interaction between the family workers and crèche workers to share information on concerns and successes in relation to children's progress and learning in the crèches at the regular family review meetings chaired by the senior family worker.

The introduction of regular supervision of the crèche workers allowed Anna to explain the processes she wanted staff to follow and offer individual coaching where the staff required this support. Anna also encouraged the staff to engage more closely with parents, explaining what the children had been doing when they attended the crèche and how parents could extend children's engagement with learning at home, something that did not come naturally to some parents. This was also reported to family workers who were able to follow this up with parents during home visits.

A further development was the introduction of the Every Child a Talker (ECaT) programme at the children's centre in response to local concerns from schools and the children's centre about the low levels of communication, particularly spoken language displayed by children on entry to school. The ECaT programme and associated activities were incorporated into the centre's working processes.

The outcome of this approach, where high standards of input were expected for all children regardless of how small their engagement with the crèche, along with a greater linking together of all aspects of the children's centre's practice in working with children and families, led to more confident practitioners, particularly the sessional crèche staff and more holistic assessments of progress of children across the children's centre.

purpose to all the stakeholders, but within this there may be other factors which impinge the frequency that practitioners need supervision sessions. For example, might staff who have regular front-line experiences with families and family support need to meet more regularly than, say, administrative staff? Might less experienced workers require more regular supervision sessions (where what is provided might possibly overlap more or flow seamlessly with mentoring or coaching needs)? Might practitioners who have not been employed for a long time by this particular setting (regardless of their overall experience) require more regular supervision (for example, perhaps overlapping with induction) at least in the early stages of their employment?

The Tickell Review comments:

> within all early years settings, supervision should be intrinsic to effective leadership and management practice, which means leaders and managers need to have the necessary skills and training . . . Supervision should be expressed in such a way that encourages reflective practice and moves away from the perception that it is merely a tick-box approach to check what practitioners are, or are not, doing. (Department for Education, 2011, p. 47)

We are reminded here of the importance of leaders, the skills they hold, their capacity to listen, to 'hold' and 'contain' emotions and feelings and anxieties, and to move their staff towards effective and quality provision and practice. A key question then might be 'Who does this for the leader?' and this brings us to the role of external support and the possibilities this might bring to providing professional support and quality enhancement for the setting leader.

Support from outside the setting: early years networks

Settings can gain support from a range of existing networks, either national (such as, for example, the National Day Nurseries Asociation (NDNA), Tactyc, Early Education and the National Children's Bureau (NCB)) or local; for example, those initially set up and convened by local authority advisors or childminder network co-ordinators. These are ways of sharing and developing communities of practice (Wenger, 1998) and keeping notions of quality on the agenda. The idea of such support groups offering peer-to-peer opportunities to help each other and themselves in reflecting on practice issues is currently held in high esteem and has become more valued as reducing local authority budgets and responsibility for quality has shifted. The introduction of early years teaching schools in recent years, with their brief for developing and enhancing professionalism across the sector, has brought another opportunity for localized quality development and professional support for practitioners. In place of the local authority almost being the sole provider of training and support in the development of quality provision, the expectation is that in future the approach is more sector-led and tailored to local priorities identified by practitioners and leaders rather than local authority advisers.

Reflection point 4.5

How, as a practitioner or leader, do you access support from outside the setting? How do networks or communities of practice enhance the quality of your work and that of the team?

Conclusion

The changing face of support, with the shift from a model of local authority support to locally developed networks, possibly focused on specific aspects of delivering quality provision, has required settings to become more self-reliant. It has opened up the possibilities for providers to focus on developing alliances to drive improvement and provide CPD opportunities that are relevant and responsive to the needs of leaders, practitioners and ultimately the children and their families served by the early years sector. For settings to achieve good outcomes, the need for quality support for all staff and a need to sustain positive relationships is essential. Leaders will need to be creative and determined to ensure they maximize the learning and development opportunities they source for themselves, their teams and the children and families in their care.

References

Brownlee, J., & Berthelsen, D. (2006). Personal epistemology and relational pedagogy in early childhood teacher education programs. *Early Years, 26*(1), 17–29.

Bubb, S., & Earley, P. (2007). *Leading and managing continuing professional development* (2nd ed.). London: Paul Chapman.

Coleyshaw, L., Whitmarsh, J., Jopling, M., & Hadfield, M. (2013). *Listening to Children's Perspectives: Improving the quality of provision in early years settings (Research Report 239B)*. Wolverhampton: Department for Education and CeDARE, University of Wolverhampton.

Dahlberg, G., Moss, P., & Pence, A. (2007). *Beyond quality in early childhood education and care: Languages of evaluation* (2nd ed.). London: Routledge.

Department for Children, Schools and Families. (2008). *Statutory framework for the early years foundation stage*. London: DCSF.

Department for Education. (2011). *The early years: Foundations for life, health and learning—an independent report on the early years foundation stage to Her Majesty's government (Tickell Review).* London: DfE.

Department for Education. (2012). *Foundations for quality: The independent review of early education and childcare qualifications (Nutbrown Report).* London: DfE.

Department for Education. (2013). *More great childcare: Raising quality and giving parents more choice.* London: DfE.

Department for Education. (2014). *Statutory framework for the early years foundation stage.* London: DfE.

Department for Education. (2015) *Special Educational Needs & Disability Code of Practice.* London: Crown Copyright.

Department for Education and Skills. (2002). *Birth to three matters.* London: DfES.

Department for Education and Skills. (2006). *The early years foundation stage: Consultation on a single quality framework for services for children birth to three.* Nottingham: DfES.

Dewey, J. (1910). *How we think.* Boston, MA: D.C. Heath.

Dunn, J. (2004). *Children's friendships: The beginnings of intimacy.* Oxford: Blackwell.

Dunn, J. (1988). *The beginnings of social understanding.* Oxford: Blackwell.

Edgington, M. (2004) *The Foundation Stage Teacher in Action.* London: Paul Chapman Publishing.

Elfer, P., & Dearnley, K. (2007). Nurseries and emotional well being: Evaluating an emotionally containing model of continuing professional development. *Early Years, 27*(3), 267–279.

Elfer, P., Goldschmied, E., & Selleck, D. Y. (2012). *Key persons in the early years: Building relationships for quality provision in early years settings and primary schools* (2nd ed.). Abingdon: Routledge.

Fitzgerald, D. (2004). *Parent Partnerships in the early years.* London: Continuum.

Georgeson, J., Campbell-Barr, V., Mathers, S., Boag-Munroe, G., Parker-Rees, R., & Caruso, F. (2014). *2-year-olds in England: An exploratory study.* Retrieved on June 1, 2015 from http://tactyc.org.uk/research/.

Gerhardt, S. (2004). *Why love matters: How affection shapes a baby's brain.* London: Routledge.

Goldschmeid, E., & Jackson, S. (2003). *People under three: Young children in day care.* London: Routledge.

Goleman, D., Boyzatis, R., & McKee, A. (2002). *The new leaders.* London: Time Warner.

Guile, D., & Lucas, N. (1999). Rethinking initial teacher education and professional development in further education: Towards the learning professional. In A.

Green & N. Lucas (Eds.), *Further education and lifelong learning: Realigning the sector for the twenty-first century*. London: Institute of Education.

Johns, C. (2004). *Becoming a reflective practitioner* (2nd ed.). Oxford: Blackwell.

Lindon, J., & Lindon, L. (2011). *Leadership and early years professionalism*. Abingdon: Hodder.

Malaguzzi, L. (1998). History, ideas and basic philosophy. In C. Edwards, L. Gandini, & G. Forman (Eds.), *The hundred languages of children* (pp. 49–97). Norwood: Ablex.

Manning-Morton, J., & Thorp, M. (2015). *2-year-olds in early years settings: Journeys of discovery*. Maidenhead: Open University Press.

Moyles, J. (2006). *Effective leadership and management in the early years*. Maidenhead: Open University Press.

Muijs, D., Aubrey, C., Harris, A., & Briggs, M. (2004). How do they manage? A review of the research on leadership in early childhood. *Journal of Early Childhood Research, 2*(2), 157–169.

Office for Standards in Education, Children's Services and Skills. (2011). *School governance: Learning from the best*. London: Ofsted.

Office for Standards in Education, Children's Services and Skills. (2012). *Evaluation schedule for inspections of registered early years provision: Guidance and grade descriptors for inspecting registered early years provision from September 2012*. London: Ofsted.

Rodd, J. (2006). *Leadership in early childhood* (3rd ed.). Maidenhead: Oxford University Press.

Rogoff, B. (1990). *Apprenticeship in thinking*. Oxford: Oxford University Press.

Sammons, P., Hillman, J., & Mortimore, P. (1999). *Key characteristics of effective schools*. London: Institute of Education.

Senge, P. (2006). *The fifth discipline*. London: Random House.

Siraj-Blatchford, I. (2009). Early childhood education (ECE). In T. Maynard & N. Thomas (Eds.), *An Introduction to early childhood studies* (2nd ed., pp. 148–160). London: Sage.

Siraj-Blatchford, I., & Hallett, E. (2014). *Effective and caring leadership in the early years*. London: Sage.

Siraj-Blatchford, I., Sylva, K., Muttock, K., Gilden, R., & Bell, D. (2002). *Researching effective pedagogy in the early years*. London: Department of Education and Skills (DfES).

Sylva, K., Melhuish, E., Sammons, P., Siraj-Blatchford, I., & Taggart, B. (2004). *The effective provision of pre-school education (EPPE) project: Final report. A longitudinal study funded by the DfES 1997–2004*. London: Department for Education and Skills (DfES).

Vygotsky, L. (1978). *Mind in society: The development of higher psychological processes.* Cambridge, MA: Harvard University Press.

Wenger, E. (1998). *Communities of practice: Learning, meaning and identity.* Cambridge: Cambridge University Press.

Whalley, M. (2008). *Involving parents in their children's learning* (2nd ed.). London: Paul Chapman.

Wheeler, H., & Connor, J. (2009). *Parents, early years and learning: Parents as partners in the early years foundation stage.* London: National Children's Bureau.

5 Quality in the early years curriculum

Perry Knight

According to Soler and Miller (2003, p. 57) 'curricula can become sites of "struggle" between ideas about what early education is for, and what are appropriate content and contexts for learning and development in early childhood'. In earlier chapters we explored how fundamentally different ideas about the purposes of early education are enacted in ideas of what constitutes quality: in practice, in training and in the design of learning environments, to name but a few.

A high-quality early childhood curriculum will have a profound and lasting effect on how children learn and how they enjoy the process of their learning (Stacey, 2009). The curriculum has the power to transform concepts of learning for a young child and start the child on a successful, albeit steep, trajectory into lifelong learning. Developing a curriculum involves providing a framework that deconstructs skills, knowledge and understanding and mapping them against specific learning and developmental outcomes. These have to be reconstructed in specific pedagogical practices that support meaningful activities for young children. This definition suggests that a good curriculum is more than an entitlement defined in terms of activities, experiences or outcomes, but instead is a critical tool in the development of learning dispositions and identities. In Chapter 4 we discussed how the learning environment could best be seen through the lens of 'potentiating' learning dispositions. The same applies to the curricular activities that we offer, transforming tacit and invisible values into practices that are explicit and visible (Claxton, 2011). This turns the curriculum from something abstract and distant into the basis of learning conversations and relationships between the young child and their family, peers and teachers.

As a child progresses through their school career and matures, learning develops from effective dyadic relationships with others that offer correction, mutual support, encouragement and guidance, to extended learning relationships that include peers, and group relationships, where the outcome is to participate within a range of contexts.

According to Kozulin (1986, p. 13), while Piaget argues that a preschool child is unable to decentre, but has the ability to absorb meaning through discovery and play, Vygotsky stresses that the importance learning occurs not through experience with things, but through using language; a distinction also explored by Minick (2005). This is not a simple dichotomy, however, as Vygotsky also views play, fantasy and games as important activities for cognitive, motivational and social development (Bronfenbrenner, 1979, p. 52). If play is such an essential ingredient to the development of learning in early childhood, then why can it not be used throughout a child's education to foster confidence, participation and self-confidence? If we look at the way in which curricula are structured and particularly at how learning is assessed, it can be argued that schools neglect play as an element of learning and, therefore, potentially tame or even limit imagination.

Stacey (2009) suggests that young children have an 'inborn curiosity' that enables them to explore, experience and express learning within a variety of contexts and as a result have an innate urge to want to learn and think more. They examine the unexamined, continually building on their existing knowledge (this is one of the challenges we discussed in Chapter 4 in the context of how to change learning environments continually to offer challenge and opportunities. These habits and dispositions may be in tension with the curriculum and its associated pedagogical practices. Even though a wide range of research has identified how educational provision needs to foster creativity and be individualized for all young children, these may be subjugated to the demands of what Dowling (2014) calls the 'hurry along' curriculum, designed to address requirements for raised standards in early literacy and early numeracy.

This raises significant questions when defining quality early years education; in particular, whether the early years curriculum is in danger of becoming a prescribed, repetitive provision promoting attainment-based concepts and skills in preparation for school readiness rather than something that allows children to develop curiosity, imagination and resilience. In this chapter, we consider the meaning of quality within differing curriculum settings and the tensions between policies; desirable outcomes for early childhood; and the interpretation of local and individual models.

The historical context

Prior to 1988, there was no statutory control on the primary school curriculum and it was argued that curricula based on topic work lacked structure and continuity and thus hindered progress for a child (Her Majesty's Stationery Office, 1985). To support curriculum continuity and progression, the 1988 National Curriculum defined what was perceived as a child-centred approach to delivery and assessment while providing a sequence of meaningful learning from primary to secondary school (Lawton, 1997). Accompanying these curriculum reforms was the introduction of assessment of key subject objectives for children aged 7, 11, 14 and 16, including external testing in the 'core' subjects of English, mathematics and science.

Wyse, McCreery, and Torrance (2008, p. 11) explain how they identified four key aspects arrangements contained within education reform of the 1980s (Department of Education and Science, 1987), namely:

- ensuring that all pupils study a broad and balanced range of subjects
- setting clear objectives for what children should be able to achieve
- ensuring that all pupils have access to the same programmes of study which include key content, skills and processes that they need to learn
- checking on progress towards those objectives and performance at various stages

The introduction of the national curriculum impacted on early years practice, not only in its content (in that many providers based their curriculum on the subjects of the primary national curriculum), but also through the explicit and implicit ideas of quality outlined above. While the broad curricular aim was of holistically developing skills, knowledge and understanding, this was accompanied by 'hurry along' assessments and led Soler and Miller (2003, p. 66) to define the emergent 'foundation stage' as an example of a 'centralized, competence-oriented curriculum'. Against this background debate began around the purpose of formal and informal learning; the role of play; the acknowledgement of cultural differences in early childhood; and the broader purpose of early years education that we see today.

The landmark Effective Provision of Pre-School Education (EPPE) project, discussed in Chapter 1), explored young children's preschool experience and enhancement of their cognitive, physical, linguistic, social and emotional development. To reiterate, EPPE and its associated projects concluded that:

- preschool experience, compared with none, enhances all-round development in children
- high-quality preschooling is related to better intellectual, as well as social and behavioural development for children
- where settings view educational and social development as complementary and equal in importance, children make better all-round progress. (Sammons et al., 2004; Sylva, Melhuish, Sammons, Siraj-Blatchford, & Taggart, 2004)

In addition, the project stated that 'preschool workers' knowledge of the particular curriculum area that is being addressed is 'just as important in the early years as it is at any later stage of education' (Sammons et al., 2004, p. 6). This is a view that goes far beyond the notion of early years as 'childcare', and demands that within early childhood education it is essential that the curriculum not only provides a framework of learning in which young children can actively participate, but also that teachers are confident and competent to deliver it.

The nature of the early years curriculum

The early years curriculum does not necessarily replicate school experience, but is better thought of as a way of process of helping children to deepen their understanding by articulating, exploring and revisiting their experiences, thoughts and ideas. Bruner wrote: 'We begin with the hypothesis that any subject can be taught in some intellectually honest form to any child at any stage of development' (1960, p. 33). Even young children, with the aid of an adult, have the ability to deconstruct and construct meaning through a 'spiral curriculum' in which ideas are revisited, challenged and elaborated. Learning, rather than simply involving acquisition and cumulation ('building up') of knowledge, is seen as a voyage of discovery that is explored, directed and experienced in a variety of forms and contexts; successful participation within a successful learning partnership fosters confidence and maintains curiosity, ultimately allowing children to continue this process on their own or initiate it with others.

So how does the Early Years Foundation Stage (EYFS) address this aim? The EYFS is a statutory framework that was developed in order to ensure consistency across all settings in terms of provision, a foundation to lifelong learning and raising standards for all young children. At the same time it acknowledges the huge trajectory of a child's learning from birth to 5 years old; recognizes that children are unique, developing and learning at different rates and in different ways; and highlights the importance of quality relationships and environments (as we have discussed in other chapters).

So here is the challenge: once a curriculum is tied to measurement against prescribed outcomes, how can that measurement or assessment be flexible enough to capture individual experiences and learning trajectories? And can the ideal of a holistic and individualized curriculum be maintained? More significantly for current early year practice, does the EYFS enable this or prevent it; or is it up to teachers to work within the broad framework of the EYFS in order to provide a curriculum that is locally relevant, holistic and personalized?

With its emphasis on measurement, progress and 'development', as well as the strong suggestion of preparation and 'readiness' for the next stage of schooling, there are implicit parallels with Piaget's theories detailing stages of cognitive development (1954). Outcomes of EYFS detail 'expected' norms for children of different ages: Piaget considers that a child between birth and 2 years old has the ability to use memory and thought to develop a greater understanding of the context in which they are in. Within this sensorimotor stage, the child will begin to understand that objects do exist when hidden, for example. In addition, a child will move from reflex actions to more goal-directed activities. A child's cognitive development through the subsequent pre-operational, concrete operational and formal operational stages involves developments in the use of language, thought, and social expectations in conversation, issues and self-identity (Table 5.1).

While an attainment-based curriculum designed around prescriptive activities may prepare a child for school, careful consideration is required to ensure the

Table 5.1: Piaget's Stages of Development

Stage	Age	Characteristics
Sensorimotor	Birth to 2	The very young child: • begins to make use of imitation, memory, thought • begins to recognize that objects do not cease to exist when they are hidden • moves from reflex actions to goal-directed activity
Pre-operational	2 to 7	The young child: • gradually develops use of language and ability to think in symbolic form • is able to think operations through logically in one direction • has difficulty seeing another person's point of view
Concrete operational	7 to 11	The child: • is able to solve concrete (hand-on) problems in a logical way • understands laws of conservation and is able to classify and put things in order • understands reversibility
Formal operational	11 to adult	The young person: • is able to solve abstract problems in logical way • becomes more scientific in thinking • develops concerns about social issues and identity

Source: *Adapted from Woolfolk, Hughes, and Walkup (2013)*

philosophy of the EYFS is endorsed that centres on the holistic development of the child. It is essential that the curriculum encourages exploration, social learning and fulfils the essential requirements of early literacy and numeracy, all of which have to be integrated within the developing child's unique learning journey.

Linkage between Piaget and EYFS identifies expected age-appropriate developmental outcomes. However, the organization of a curriculum based on intended learning outcomes or assessment standards is in danger of diminishing an early years curriculum that is individualized to suit a child's developmental needs.

Reflection point 5.1

Consider the following questions:

- What are the similarities and differences between the characteristics and outcomes of Piaget's stages of cognitive development and the early years outcomes?
- How are aspects of the curricula with which you have worked mapped to age-related developmental and learning outcomes?
- How do these curricula identify targets or promote 'next steps' within a child's development and learning? Are these in relation to age or learning outcomes?

Going deeper: curriculum models

There are many international perspectives on early childhood education, and these are reflected in curricula and frameworks, though all locate the child as the focus of learning and, therefore, the curriculum, to some extent. Consider Bronfenbrenner's (1979) conceptualization of a 'Russian doll' in which the child is at the heart: as a child develops, sociocultural factors begin to shape and mould a child's learning and development, thus a child becomes consumed in layers of influence. The curriculum, as one of the means by which these sociocultural factors are expressed, is one way in which the child's development is framed and guided, and may be enabled or constrained.

Similarly, other conceptions of what quality early years education involves have different perspectives on how the curriculum should be thought about. The Reggio Emilia approach (which we have already discussed) is a complex system founded on collaboration among children, teachers and parents; the co-construction of knowledge; the interdependence of individual and social learning; and the role of culture in understanding this interdependence (Rankin, 2004). This means that the curriculum, rather than being based around the child acquiring knowledge, sees them as already equipped to participate and engage in developing potential and rationalizing existing knowledge. The Te Whāriki early years curriculum of New Zealand (New Zealand Ministry of Education, 2014) is explicitly sociocultural in its outlook and sees the child at the heart of the family and wider community. Its curriculum is founded on dialogic engagement whereby a child will talk with others including their peers and teachers, and considers the child's environment to be vitally important, allowing a freedom to explore and actively participate in community activities. Reflecting on Emilia Reggio and Te Whāriki, we can see that their approaches, which are seen as being high quality or even exemplary, are underpinned by holistic views and learning and offer curricula that promote desirable outcomes enabling young children not just to achieve pre-scribed targets, but also to access and develop individualized learning identities.

Carr and Lee (2012) identify that successful learning relationships are those in which the teacher can motivate, sustain and positively challenge young chil-dren so that each child is ready, willing and able to participate in a variety of learning contexts. We can think of the curriculum as providing the framework within which these relationships can be developed. So a curriculum that is framed largely in terms of progression towards targets, rather than the kinds of holis-tic sociocultural aims outlined above may limit the potential for these relation-ships to develop. However, Hedges, and Cooper (2014) question whether the EYFS offers holistic outcomes for all young children.

So what can early years teachers do in practice to enhance curriculum pro-vision and support positive learning relationships? Bruce (2011, p. 207) identifies four areas. The first is the role played by assessment to measure a child's progress through developmental outcomes and learning. This is closely linked to the sec-ond, evaluation of the child's experience in their setting and curriculum content. Evaluation provides detailed feedback of strategies and learning contexts that promote individualized learning. The third is described as 'retro-forward planning'. This involves consistently examining what the child has been doing; what the child is interested in; and what the child has recently engaged with. Finally, Bruce stresses the importance of a record-keeping system that aligns with the philosophy of the educational setting, and suggests that if records do not reflect the principles of the setting, then this will, in turn, misdirect practice. What is important about this is that outcomes are not seen as a prescriptive set of criteria that are somehow external to or separate from the setting and the learning that takes place within it, but rather are an account of a child's initial learning journey, immersed in the con-text of the preschool setting. For example, a learning journey portfolio documents a child's learning progress within a setting through photographs, observations and examples of a child's work. This document is shared between setting and carer. However, in a setting inspired by Reggio Emilia, approaches would document the discussions, the direction that a child's enquiry had taken, and the various cultural elements that had impacted it. Therefore, the result would be a portfolio of learn-ing, rather than presenting a product of a child's activities.

Quality curricula within the EYFS framework

In providing a quality curriculum, it is important to recognize that the EYFS does not represent the totality of the learning experience of the child. Hedges and Cooper (2014) question whether the EYFS itself is a guarantee of holistic experience and outcomes for all children. Between this framework for consistent provision and the day-to-day activities of the learner lie a range of curricular models, which may reflect different educational philosophies, cultural expectations and pedagogical models. We can see the curriculum as an 'enactment' or 'translation' of different intentions on the part of different stakeholders, some of whom will have competing ideas about what 'matters' in early education. The curriculum may become an uncomfortable 'hybrid' (trying to address competing aims and purposes) or, as suggested right at the beginning of this chapter, a 'site of struggle' (Soler & Miller, 2003).

So let us now examine the EYFS in order to explore how quality early education might be provided within its framework. The EYFS is already something of a 'hybrid' in that it identifies three *characteristics of effective teaching and learning*:

- Playing and exploring: children investigate and experience things, and 'have a go'.
- Active learning: children concentrate and keep on trying if they encounter difficulties, and enjoy achievements;
- Creating and thinking critically: children have and develop their own ideas, make links between ideas, and develop strategies for doing things. (Department for Education, 2014, p. 9)

And seven *strands of learning* (probably very familiar if you have spent time in early years settings!), three of which are the 'prime areas of learning':

- communication and language
- physical development
- personal, social and emotional development

And four of which are the 'specific areas of learning':

- literacy
- mathematics
- understanding the world
- expressive arts and design

The strands are subdivided for assessment purposes into 17 targets, achievement of a combination of which is taken as an indicator of a 'good level of development': that Piagetian model of staged development being 'reasserted', regardless of the actual philosophy, curriculum or practice that may characterize the particular setting.

Reflection point 5.2

The EYFS (Department for Education, 2014) provides a statutory framework for the curriculum offer within your setting. Consider how your setting has interpreted this offer to the children you support, including your key children within your setting. You might need to reflect on:

- the overarching principles of the EYFS
- the three characteristics of effective teaching and learning
- the seven strands of learning

As you consider the areas of the EYFS, you might also ask yourself how your setting:

- defines quality in the curriculum offered, as distinct from other aspects of provision
- promotes active learning opportunities and then how it assesses them
- shares your curriculum approach with other stakeholders including parents and carers, primary schools and other local providers and services

---

Developing quality through curricular practice

What we have been developing in this chapter is a view that quality in the curriculum is based not solely on the statutory framework that governs early years provision and practice, nor the targets that the children are intended to reach. Rather, such frameworks provide a statement of the expected experience of children across all settings that can be adapted and localized within individual settings. These then develop an 'intended curriculum' informed by a particular ethos or philosophy and it is the job of teachers to use their pedagogical expertise and experience to apply and adapt this in the light of individual children's needs, interests and motivations. According to this perspective, quality is a matter of the interpretation and not the execution of a standardized framework.

In the final section of this chapter we will consider a number of approaches that might inform this interpretation at setting or individual level. Soler and Miller (2003) describe how considering differing models of the curriculum can develop holistic, individualized learning. Each of these represents a way of navigating the 'space' between the overarching structures of the EYFS and its associated assessment processes and the experiences of the individual children in a setting. They characterize 'emergent', 'progressive', 'evolving' and 'play-based' models.

The emergent curriculum

Stacey (2009) identifies that the voice of the child is integral to an emergent curriculum model. Therefore, development and learning is child-initiated involving collaboration between the child and adult. Child-led activities actively promote curiosity and questioning allowing the child to make decisions through enquiry and self-direction. The emergent curriculum develops a close relationship between the concepts of a child's prior knowledge influencing new individual and social learning experiences.

The progressive curriculum

A progressive curriculum has greater emphasis on a child's learning journey, rather than explicitly detailing curriculum content. Therefore, a child-centred approach offers a more structured approach to a child's learning, rather than the potential informality of child-led activities. Soler and Miller (2003) define a progressive curriculum as one in which teachers make imaginative use of space that invite a variety of learning opportunities and allow a child to continually engage within a variety of learning roles. However, the emergent and progressive curriculum models are often interchangeable, as a teacher can establish a child-centred learning environment in which children can then lead and self-direct activities.

Vignette: The emergent-progressive curriculum in action

Anne, an early years teacher and Forest School leader, leads a small preschool within a village community. The preschool has very good links with the village primary school and other schools within the local area. There are a variety of learning areas within the preschool including a vegetable and flower garden, soft play and dry/water play areas. Behind the preschool is a small 'forest' in which a Forest School has been recently established.

Anne has identified areas in which curriculum development would benefit the learning experience of young children. This encompasses a child-centred approach using EYFS as a framework to assess developmental and learning outcomes. The preschool offers a child-centred approach in which children's choice is the foundation to planning. Its ethos is one of nurturing, caring and ensuring all children aspire to learn. Therefore, she developed spaces for children to engage in child-initiated and child-centred learning. This includes the Forest School, which is informed by a progressive curriculum model (Soler & Miller, 2003). It includes opportunities for children to further experience and explore the outside; to develop social and individualized learning; and to holistically engage with teacher planned opportunities. These 'natural' resources and activities involve a fire-pit, shelter building and pond dipping.

To launch this new learning space, the preschool devised a topic-led curriculum project based on 'The Bear Hunt'. This promoted the concept of bringing the outdoors in. Within the preschool a bear cave was created for a quiet area. Displays celebrated children's work from their nature trails, collages and leaf rubbing. Children were introduced to the forest by going on a 'bear hunt' that accumulated into story-time within the forest's story circle and having lunch cooked on the forest pit. These activities, with their emphasis on child-centred experience and development, align with a progressive model of the curriculum.

As children develop greater confidence in their new learning area, child-initiated activities emerged. Children developed choice based on prior experience. For example, from forest activities children initiated their own learning through leaf collection, building shelters, climbing trees and role play. Children freely moved between their own learning experience and resources available to them.

In addition to the displays of forest activities throughout the setting, children's learning is documented by photographs, examples of work and practitioner observations in individual learning journeys. Progress is continually mapped against EYFS outcomes with next steps clearly documented.

The evolving curriculum

The rapid emergence of new digital technologies, argue Aubrey and Dahl (2008, p. 15), demands that young children become 'digitally literate' and have access to an early years curriculum where they can use Information Communications Technology (ICT) to access and enhance their learning, particularly through the 'understanding of the world' area of learning of the EYFS. According to this perspective, quality in an early years curriculum has to respond the needs of individuals and society on an international, national and local landscape. An exciting and challenging aspect of curriculum development is that teachers are aiding the development of young children to engage with resources, activities and employment opportunities that do not yet exist; with the speed of technological development the curricula evolves and educational journeys are ever more unpredictable. Hence, early years settings may contain voice recorders, laptops and handheld computers, use of the email, Powerpoint and Internet, DVDs, digital cameras, 'walkie-talkies' and 'smart' toys, dance mats, camcorders, electronic microscopes, robots, interactive whiteboards, touch screens and CCTV (Siraj-Blatchford & Siraj-Blatchford, 2006).

Within a few years, a new raft of technologies may have emerged: watch out for eyegaze systems for computer control, motion and gesture recognition and 'intelligent bricks' – toys that can be combined creatively so that children can build their own 'small worlds' with programmable inhabitants and objects. A quality curriculum ensures that emergent technologies are explored between the child and practitioner. This is achieved by ensuring technology forms a central resource in planning. In addition, the practitioner and child experiment with technologies. For example, the digital cameras used to document a child's progress can be used by children themselves to take photographs and collate records of their own work and activities.

There are certain practical considerations that teachers need to take into account in such technology-rich environments and dilemmas to be addressed. The first is the impact of 'screen time' in which young children play with computer-based systems to support learning. It is essential that young children initiate these learning opportunities, and teachers develop child-centred approaches to consolidate understanding rather than these being a mandatory or highly structured part of the daily routine. The second is the need to develop good practice both from the teacher and child viewpoint: exploring technologies requires confidence and understanding, and any curriculum that incorporates digital technologies needs to demonstrate how these promote the development of social learning as well as early digital literacy and numeracy.

The play-based curriculum

The fourth model is the play-based curriculum. In many ways, this encapsulates a variety of developments and promotes a range of learning opportunities for young children. Stacey (2009) suggests that play-based learning is self-chosen and self-directed by the child and, therefore, constitutes a fully inclusive framework for settings. However, play is complex and for a play-based model to derive learning opportunities, a teacher needs to know how a child plays in order for the curriculum to address statutory requirements and stakeholder expectations.

Dau (1999, p. 67) identifies play as a learned behaviour, acquired as children interact with older members of the society in which they live. Play allows a child to develop imagination through pretend and fantasy play and characterizations for other children with which to socially interact. Play also develops physical, social and emotional well-being by 'locomotor' play that may involve changing characterizations in which children innately adapt from being 'chased' to 'chaser' (Jarvis, 2013).

A play-based curriculum, then, has the potential to engage with all strands of learning within the EYFS curriculum, and as we have discussed, play is validated within the EYFS as being an essential strategy to promote active engagement and learning. However, a play-based curriculum proposes challenges to settings and play may be restricted due to choice of resources and limitation within classroom settings. Some settings may have a 'zero tolerance' policy in which play can be deemed as 'rough and tumble', rather than responding to some missed opportunities developed by other children. Despite such challenges, a quality play-based curriculum has the capacity for children and practitioners to enact and experience what is intended as an inclusive entitlement.

Vignette: The emergent-play-based curriculum in action

Jack and Emma are 4 years old and attend a local village preschool with a Forest School attached. The children love to explore the outdoors, especially in the forest area. Their favourite game is hide-and-seek. Recently, the preschool invested in a set of walkie-talkies. The devices are used extensively by the children indoors and out.

During a forest activity in which children are tracking animal prints in the soil, Jack and Emma have taken the walkie-talkies into the forest and are using the devices to talk to each other. They talk about what they see and Jack says that he sees a large animal, which could be a 'dinosaur'. He whispers into the walkie-talkie describing its height, colour and its very big feet. Jack tells Emma that they need to hide in the shelter to escape from the Dinosaur. Emma hides in a shelter that was previously built and tells Jack that she is safe. Jack counts to '10' and tells Emma that he will find her before the dinosaur does!

Conclusion

EYFS (Department for Education, 2014) is a nationally 'directed' model that provides explicit outcomes for young children. This is the 'intended' curriculum. However, a quality curriculum encompasses a range of models according to the requirements of the setting and child. Its quality, directed from EYFS, is to provide nationally benchmarked outcomes, but its interpretation may be derived from a variety of sources including an emergent, progressive, evolving and play-based curriculum. Each model should not stand alone, but should be intertwined to maximize the experience of active learning, therefore, determining a definition of quality that places considerable pressure on early years teachers. The role of the early years teacher is twofold. The first is to be attentive to an individual child's needs. The second is to be pedagogically knowledgeable. Each of these feeds into establishing an exciting and relevant curriculum that supports the child through the foundations of their early learning.

In response to the question opening this chapter, 'when defining quality, is the early years curriculum in danger of becoming prescribed and an inherited repetitive provision promoting attainment-based concepts and skills in preparation for school readiness?', we can argue that learning is about developing knowledge, identity and self-belief in understanding wider concepts of the world. Within learning, subjects give boundaries and teachers have the power to transform children's enquiring minds. They can create knowledge that is both powerful and can develop social identities of children. However, any response also needs to consider the impact of the national agenda of the EYFS on localized curriculum policies. Quality is not about a best-fit scenario for the setting; it is about improving life changes for young children. Children have a right to engage actively within their curriculum and to develop their inborn curiosity. They have a right to develop and learn. Therefore, teachers have to challenge through their practice the assumption that the 'intended' curriculum is the only curriculum. A quality curriculum injects excitement for learning; flexibility in learning; explicit tools to support child development; and ensuring positive learning relationships between children, their families and their setting.

Reflection point 5.3

This chapter considers the role and purpose of a quality curriculum within early years settings. By doing so, it raises questions about its definition and relationship to the EYFS. Consider the varying curriculum models your setting offers and reflect on:

- How do teachers reconcile the demands of the EYS with personal beliefs and those of stakeholders?
- How does the curriculum reflect the ethos in your setting?
- Which of the models discussed do you observe in your setting? How do you know?
- When planning your next activity, which curriculum model will help you structure it? Evaluate the outcome of the activity.

References

Aubrey, C., & Dahl, S. (2008). *A review of the evidence on the use of ICT in the Early Years Foundation Stage.* Warwick: University of Warwick: Becta.

Bronfenbrenner, U. (1979). *The ecology of human development: Experiments by nature and design.* Cambridge, MA: Harvard University Press.

Bruce, T. (2011). Early childhood education (4th ed.). London: Hodder.

Bruner, J. (1960). *The process of education.* Cambridge, MA: Harvard University Press.

Carr, M., & Lee, W. (2012) *Learning stories: Constructing learner identities in early education.* London: Sage.

Claxton, G. (2011). *The learning powered school: Pioneering 21st century education.* Bristol: The Learning Organisation.

Dau, E. (Ed.). (1999). *Child's play: Revisiting play in early childhood settings.* Sydney: Maclennan and Petty.

Department for Education. (2014). *Statutory framework for the Early Years Foundation Stage.* London: DfE.

Department for Education and Science/Welsh Office. (1987). *The national curriculum 5–16: A consultative document.* London: DfES/Welsh Office.

Dowling, M. (2014). *Young children's personal and emotional development* (4th ed.). London: Sage.

Hedges, H., & Cooper, M. (2014). Engaging with holistic curriculum outcomes: deconstructing 'working theories'. *International Journal of Early Years Education, 22*(4), 395–408.

Her Majesty's Stationery Office (1985) *Education 8 to 12 in combined and middle schools: A survey by HM Inspector of Schools.* London: HMSO.

Jarvis, P. (2013). Born to play: The biocultural roots of rough and tumble play, and its impact upon young children's learning and development. In P. Broadhead, J. Howard, & E. Wood (Eds.), *Play and learning in the early years.* London: Sage.

Kozulin, A. (1986). *Thought and language by Lev Vygotsky.* Cambridge MA: The MIT Press.

Lawton, D. (1987). What is worth learning? In R. Pring and G. Walford (Eds.), *Affirming the comprehensive ideal* (pp. 99–108). London: Falmer Press.

Minick, N. (2005). The development of Vygotsky's thought: An introduction to thinking and speech. In H. Daniels (Ed.), *An introduction to Vygotsky* (pp. 33–59). London: Routledge.

New Zealand Ministry of Education. (2014). *Early childhood education: Te Whāriki.* Retrieved 1 June, 2015, from http://www.educate.ece.govt.nz/ learning/curriculumAndLearning/TeWhariki.aspx

Piaget, J. (1954). *The construction of reality in the child.* New York: Basic Books.

Rankin, B. (2004). The importance of intentional socialization among children in small groups: A conversation with Loris Malaguzzi. *Early Childhood Education Journal, 32*(2), 81–85.

Sammons, P., Sylva, K., Melhuish, E., Siraj-Blatchford, I., Taggart, B., Elliot, K., & Marsh, A. (2004). *The Effective Provision of Pre-School Education (EPPE) Project: Technical Paper 11 - The Continuing Effects of Pre-school Education at Age 7 Years.* London: Department for Education and Skills (DfES) and University of London Institute of Education.

Siraj-Blatchford, I., & Siraj-Blatchford, J. (2006). *A guide to developing the ICT curriculum for early childhood education.* Stoke-on-Trent: Trentham Books.

Soler, J., & Miller, L. (2003). The struggle for early childhood curricula: a comparison of the English foundation stage curriculum, Te Whäriki and Reggio Emilia. *International Journal of Early Years Education, 11*(1), 57–67.

Stacey, S. (2009). *Emergent curriculum in early childhood settings: From theory to practice.* St. Paul, MN: Red Leaf Press.

Sylva, K., Melhuish, E., Sammons, P., Siraj-Blatchford, I., & Taggart, B. (2004). *The Effective Provision of Pre-school Education (EPPE) Project: Final Report. A longitudinal study funded by the DfES 1997-2004*. London: Department for Education and Skills (DfES).

Woolfolk, A., Hughes, M., & Walkup, V. (2013). *Psychology in education*. Harlow: Pearson Education.

Wyse, D., McCreery, E., & Torrance, H. (2008). *The Trajectory and Impact of National Reform: Curriculum and Assessment in English Primary Schools (Primary Review Research Survey 3/2)*. Cambridge: University of Cambridge Faculty of Education.

6 Policies for quality early years provision

Sarah Cousins

This chapter revisits and extends some of the issues raised in Chapter 1, and, in particular, considers how quality is described in policy. What do national reviews and policies say about quality? To what extent do early years professionals engage with national policies? What do early years leaders need to consider when drawing up their own local policies for use in their settings? How can such setting policies enhance the quality of provision? As with the previous chapter on quality in the curriculum, we will talk a good deal about the 'mediating' role of early years professionals as they take national policy, guidance and frameworks and translate it into something that can be put into practice on a day-to-day basis.

The chapter begins with a discussion about what quality means in the context of early years policy and some of the key policy documents about quality are identified. This is followed by a discussion about the statutory framework for the Early Years Foundation Stage (EYFS), and an exploration about how settings develop their own policies for quality provision. The chapter then considers how settings can assure quality for all children, including children with special educational needs and disabilities.

Quality in early years policies: background and meanings

As we discussed in Chapter 1, the notion of quality in education came to prominence in England in educational policies when the Labour Government was in power between 1997 and 2010. The government established the Sure Start programme in 2002 and Children's Centres were set up in the most disadvantaged areas, offering high-quality multi-professional services for children and families. *Every child matters* (Her Majesty's Treasury, 2003) was introduced to establish robust, integrated working between different professionals to ensure that every child remained safe and healthy, and achieved well. Quality remained a priority after the Conservative–Liberal Democrat Coalition Government came into power in 2010. As part of a drive to reduce the complexity of policy documents, statutory requirements and guidance, *Development matters* (Early Education, 2012), for example, which contained detailed guidance for practitioners, was replaced with the *Early years outcomes* (Department for Education, 2013), which contains much more simplified outcome statements with no exemplification.

The EYFS (Department for Children, Schools and Families, 2008), with its numerous materials, was also reduced to a much slimmer framework (Department for Education, 2012b). The professional standards for primary and second-ary teachers were converted from thirty-three competence statements to eight (Department for Education, 2012c) and the following year the new Early Years Teacher Status (EYTS) was introduced with its own set of eight, specifically early years standards, to match (National College for Teaching and Leadership, 2013).

These were drives for improved 'quality' by two successive governments with different political outlooks. The idea that there is a consensus about quality, however, is contested by some authors (Dahlberg, Moss, & Pence, 2007): this is because quality is often associated with modernity and an emphasis on measura-ble outcomes over more qualitative, less measurable indicators such as emotional well-being or creative development. It is interesting, however, that the word 'qual-ity' does not appear in either the *Teachers' standards (early years)* (Department for Education, 2013) or in the *Early years outcomes* (National College for Teaching and Leadership, 2013). Rather, the teachers' standards for early years are a list of competence statements that aspiring professionals are required to meet to a good or outstanding standard in order to become early years teachers, while the early years outcomes are a list of achievements that children are expected to make, organized under the different areas of learning and development and separated into different age bands. This absence of the word 'quality' in these documents indicates that 'quality' is not something that can be 'done' by either practitioners or children. Instead, it is a desirable *feature* of education: that can permeate pro-vision in all its forms and at all stages.

Despite this, 'quality' appears both as a noun and an adjective across a range of important policies and other documents related to early years education. In the main, it is applied to provision; however, it is also adjoined to a range of specific words such as 'practice' and 'leadership'. In relation to practice, there is reference to 'quality training', 'quality learning', 'quality education', 'quality care', 'quality teaching', 'quality support' and 'quality assessments'. In relation to leadership, we find reference to 'quality leadership', 'quality data', 'quality evidence to support the quality data', 'quality settings', 'quality environments', 'quality improvement', 'quality staffing' and even 'quality places', meaning available nursery places of a particular quality.

There is an implicit understanding that quality, in all of these contexts, refers specifically to 'high' quality. So 'quality in early years', then, means some combi-nation of high-quality early years provision, practice and leadership. But 'quality' is also used as a noun: the Tickell Review of the EYFS (Department for Education, 2011) was concerned to drive up 'quality' in the early years—quality here means something that can be achieved in its own right, so that a setting or a provider might be demonstrably assessed as being of 'good quality' or 'outstanding quality'.

Quality in recent reviews of early years provision and practice

As we discussed in Chapter 1, Professor Cathy Nutbrown was commissioned by the government to look into the quality of early years provision in England and her findings were published in 2012 (Department for Education, 2012a). The report emphasized that early years practitioners are the most important determining factors in the quality of early years education and care. Children's well-being, development and achievements are directly related to the quality of those who support them; primarily, the practitioners who help them to learn through play. The review identified the main challenge facing the sector: how best can the training and qualifications system develop early years practitioners with the necessary skills, knowledge and understanding to provide quality education and care in the early years?

What the Nutbrown Review found and reported on was an early years workforce that was increasingly seeking to become more professional and knowledgeable. One of the main findings of the review was that highly qualified teams of early years practitioners were more effective in supporting children's learning and development, particularly their communication, language and literacy, reasoning, thinking and mathematical skills. The review confirmed that quality early years practitioners understood, valued and supported young children's play from babyhood and throughout their early years.

Importantly, the report suggested that practitioners with higher levels of qualification, and especially those with degree-level specialism in early childhood, had the greatest impact on children's learning and development. The review considered research on the topic and reported that graduate leaders and, in particular, qualified teachers, bring many benefits to early years settings. Graduate professionals have positive impacts on the curriculum and on children's outcomes, particularly in early literacy, social development, mathematics and science.

Despite the wealth of evidence about the benefits of high-quality early years provision, and the role of qualified staff in ensuring this, the review pointed to concerns from the sector about the standard of training available. Nutbrown pointed to a lack of understanding of the complex and important role early years practitioners undertake. The review found that working with young children involves much more than changing nappies and wiping noses. Such misconceptions, Nutbrown suggested, were unhelpful for young children whose needs are often more complex than those of older children. On a positive note, the review found many practitioners who were very proud of their work and passionate about the quality experiences they offered to young children. Many, however, also expressed concern about the lack of status afforded to their profession in society as a whole, as well as the lack of public appreciation for the work they do.

The report that emerged from the Nutbrown Review set out a practical and affordable way forward to set higher expectations and offer training for a quality workforce. As discussed in Chapter 1, not all of the recommendations that were made were welcomed, and not all found their way into government policy.

However, the report has made a strong impression on training providers, scholars and practitioners in the field.

Following the Nutbrown Review, The Sutton Trust commissioned a team at the University of Oxford to carry out a review of research evidence about quality provision for children under 3 years old, and to report of implications for policy and practice. The research evidence on which they drew identified four key dimensions of good quality pedagogy:

- stable relationships and interactions with sensitive and responsive adults
- a focus on play-based activities and routines that allow children to take the lead in their own learning
- support for communication and language
- opportunities to move and be physically active. (Mathers, Eisenstadt, Sylva, Soukakou, & Ereky-Stevens, 2014, p. 5)

Reflection point 6.1

- How do these four key dimensions of good-quality pedagogy compare with your own ideas? Is there anything in these that you did not consider? Is there anything missing?
- How could you adapt these four key dimensions designed for babies up to 2 years old so that they apply to older children of 3–5 years old?

Building on the findings of the Nutbrown Review, the Oxford University/The Sutton Trust review noted that, in order to deliver this high-quality pedagogy, practitioners should be skilled and knowledgeable and be able to work within environments that support them in their practice. The review of the research evidence (some of which we have already discussed in Chapter 1) suggested five 'key conditions' for quality:

- knowledgeable and capable practitioners, supported by strong leaders
- a stable staff team with a low turnover
- effective staff deployment (for example, favourable ratios, staff continuity)
- secure yet stimulating physical environments
- engaged and involved families. (Mathers et al., 2014, p. 5)

The report recommended that the government should implement change in the early years at a realistic pace so that policy goals, such as having more 2-year-olds in nursery, may be sustained and all children have access to good-quality provision.

The recommendations of the Nutbrown Report in relation to staff qualifications were also confirmed in the Oxford University/The Sutton Trust Review. Their report recommended that staff working with funded 2-year-olds should be qualified to at least Level 3 and have support from a graduate practitioner. Furthermore, all practitioners, including childminders, should be able to access qualifications and ongoing professional development, particularly in helping them to meet the needs of disadvantaged children and their families. The report also re-emphasized the point that salaries in the sector should be raised to reflect the requirement for higher qualifications (Mathers et al., 2014, p. 44).

Recommendations about ratios; namely, that they should remain at favourable levels (1:4 for group care settings and 1:3 for childminders) were also made

---

Reflection point 6.2

- What do you do at your work or training setting to support disadvantaged children? Is this set out in policies, or is it seen as an integral aspect of practice?

- How do you establish opportunities for children to play in mixed social groups so that disadvantaged children benefit from being with more advantaged children, as recommended by Mathers et al. (2014)?

(Mathers et al., 2014, p. 44). The report further pointed out that there should be a good social mix in early years settings so that disadvantaged children might benefit from being with more advantaged children, particularly in relation to social and language development (Mathers et al., 2014, p. 13). Finally, the report emphasized the importance of providing an appropriate physical environment for very young children.

These scholarly reviews considered research and best practice across the birth to 5 age range to arrive at recommendations for policy. But research evidence and professional views of what constitutes best practice are not the only contributors to policy, and how these reviews and their recommendations were incorporated into the EYFS and other related policy is worth considering in more detail.

The Tickell Review was commissioned to consider the EYFS and make recommendations for improvements. The review team recognized the already strong emphasis on quality relationships between settings and homes, with practitioners working in close partnership with parents and carers. However, it recommended that the government should go further, and that a greater emphasis should be given to the role of parents and carers as partners in their children's learning, and their report called for a simplified, clearer and more accessible framework. This was in order that all parties involved in children's education should be able to access it easily and work together to achieve a high-quality provision for children.

The ensuing EYFS (Department for Education, 2012b), revised in 2014 (Department for Education, 2014), states the following:

> Every child deserves the best possible start in life and the support that enables them to fulfil their potential. Children develop quickly in the early years and a child's experiences between birth and age five have a major impact on their future life chances. A secure, safe and happy childhood is important in its own right. Good parenting and high quality early learning together provide the foundation children need to make the most of their abilities and talents as they grow up. (Department for Education, 2014, Section 1)

The aims of the EYFS are stated as being to provide the following (at this point, it is interesting to consider how the word 'quality' is being used):

- quality and consistency in all early years settings, so that every child makes good progress and no child gets left behind
- a secure foundation through learning and development opportunities which are planned around the needs and interests of each individual child and are assessed and reviewed regularly
- partnership working between practitioners and with parents and/or carers
- equality of opportunity and anti-discriminatory practice, ensuring that every child is included and supported. (Department for Education, 2014, Section 1)

In order to achieve this, the framework requires an appropriately trained workforce:

> A quality learning experience for children requires a quality workforce. A well-qualified, skilled staff strongly increases the potential of any individual setting to deliver the best possible outcomes for children. (Department for Education, 2014, Section 1.11)

The framework set out the safeguarding and welfare requirements that all providers must adhere to. These were designed to help providers create

> high quality settings which are welcoming, safe and stimulating, and where children are able to enjoy learning and grow in confidence. (Department for Education, 2014, Section 3.1)

So, the notion of quality features prominently in the statutory framework for the EYFS in England. 'High quality early learning opportunities' led by a 'quality workforce', together with 'good parenting', are recommended in order that all children remain safe and well, and achieve high-quality learning experiences. Quality, then, refers to professional contexts. Interestingly, quality is constructed as a feature of settings and what they provide, rather than of homes. Parents can be 'good ', but settings and those who work in them must be of 'high quality'.

Policies in settings that promote quality provision

So, how can these national policies be transformed into effective policies and practice in early years settings? Clearly, the expectation is that 'quality leaders' must work with their 'quality staff' in order to adapt the national policies to the needs of their highly diverse contexts. In developing policies, it is important that providers pitch them appropriately. The challenge for policymakers at any level is to set policies that are neither too vague and lenient (in which case quality cannot be assured), nor too stringent, so that practitioners cease to apply their 'professional intuition' (Owen & Gillentine, 2011, p. 866) or 'professionalism from within' (Osgood, 2012, p. 131) and instead become like automata, only concerned with performing to prescribed standards. Two vignettes follow in the next section that illustrate the importance of developing and implementing flexible and clear policies that are understood and carried out by all.

Vignette: Policies about safe touch in settings

When setting policies about appropriate touch with young children, it is important not to be so prescriptive as to restrict practitioners from offering physical comfort to children when they need it. There are occasions when children benefit from a prolonged, close embrace from their key person or other significant adult.

Flori is a childminder in London. She grew up in a Latin culture and said she is accustomed to outward signs of emotion. She said that she makes it clear to parents when they choose her setting that she will show children the love they need, and that this may sometimes be expressed through touch. Flori says: 'If you are trying to be so good and outstanding with the safeguarding, and the safety, and the this and the that, you end up completely tied up in a knot and not being able to do anything.'

Ana is a nursery teacher at a large children's centre. She too said that children benefit from physical expressions of love. Ana says: 'While they are here, they're with us for a long time as well, and some children are with us from 8 until 6 so they do need that loving because otherwise, you know, for a whole day, they get nothing until they get home, and it's, it's just a long time for a three-year-old.'

So, whereas on the one hand these practitioners say that children need to be loved while in non-familial, out-of-home settings, they also say, on the other hand, that policies may be too restrictive in some cases. In the context of appropriate touch for young children, overly restrictive policies may not allow practitioners to act according to what they believe and know to be appropriate.

---

e-Safety policy in settings

It is important to have up-to-date policies that are applied by all members of staff, understood by parents and children, and have effective implementation procedures. Setting policies for online safely is an area that needs particular attention due to the increasing numbers of very young children who have access to the Internet both at home and in settings. The rapidly evolving technological landscape of online content and easy-to-use personal technologies means that regular training and updating are essential. Quality leaders need to make sure that rigorous e-safety policies and procedures are in place and that these are age-appropriate, contributed to by the whole setting and updated regularly. Quality settings need to have e-safety policies that are integrated with other relevant policies such as behaviour, safeguarding and anti-bullying, and need to be understood and implemented by all staff, not just a specific leader or curriculum co-ordinator. Quality e-safety policies incorporate:

- acceptable usage policy
- digital video and image policy
- personal device policy

Quality settings ensure that all parents as well as all staff and volunteers not only sign these, but also understand them well and apply them rigorously. Where policies are too generic, so that they do not apply to the particular context for which they are developed, or are not applied universally, they are likely to be less effective. While many settings have such policies in place, fewer of them have policies that are produced collaboratively, linked to other policies, and reviewed frequently. As policies of this kind need to be applied consistently by all staff, developing and reviewing them as a whole staff, or in consultation with other providers, represents a good way of making sure that this happens. This is 'quality policymaking' in action.

Reflection point 6.3

Think about the policymaking practices in your setting. You could start by thinking about the issue of e-safety and ask how 'quality practice' is ensured; for example by asking if:

- the e-safety policy is regularly reviewed
- there is evidence that policies are well communicated (for example, on posters, in handbooks, and so on)
- staff, volunteers and parents know the policies without going back to read them

- the policies are flexible, so that

  - children are protected
  - parents can take images at nominated events
  - the policy extends to the use of digital recording equipment and mobile technologies; for example as part of learning activities, or teacher research

You might look at other policies too and ask:

- how and by whom was this policy developed?
- how does it relate to the EYFS and other higher-level policies and frameworks? How have these been interpreted and 'mediated' into local policy and practice?
- how do these local policies steer a 'middle way' between being too vague and too stringent, while still maintaining quality provision *and practice?*

Measuring quality in the early years

Until the Conservative–Liberal Democrat Coalition Government came into power in 2010, teams of early years consultants worked for local authorities to raise quality in early years. Their remit was to drive up quality across designated geographical areas. These teams have now become much smaller and a school-to-school or setting-to-setting support model has replaced the earlier consultancy model. So, whereas until around 2011, outside bodies such as local authorities were responsible for raising quality provision in the early years, it is now leaders in settings and schools who are responsible for driving up and maintaining high-quality provision. While this is a positive move in terms of empowering teams to take responsibility for raising quality in their own settings, some settings, in their current form and due to a variety of circumstances, may still lack the capacity to self-improve without support.

It is with this in mind that Ofsted plays a key role in checking and reporting on quality provision across the early years sector. Under the common inspection framework (Ofsted, 2015) inspectors judge the quality and standards of the early years provision taking into account key judgements. These are:

- overall effectiveness
- effectiveness of the leadership and management
- quality of teaching, learning and assessment
- personal development, behaviour and welfare
- outcomes for children

Within these categories, inspectors look out for the quality of teaching and learning, the quality of the environment and the quality of standards achieved by all children. Inspectors observe and evaluate practice and match their evaluations to different criteria to arrive at their judgement.

Quality for all

Quality early years providers must have quality systems in place to support children with special educational needs or disabilities. Quality providers identify any concerns at the earliest opportunity and set up quick and effective quality provision in order to improve the outcomes of individual children.

Quality early years practitioners monitor and review the progress and development of all children in their care. Where a child's progress is behind what might be expected for their age, or gives cause for concern, quality practitioners act quickly. They consider a broad range of information about the child. In particular, they consider the child's progress across the three prime areas of learning:

- communication and language
- physical development
- personal, social and emotional development

If outside agencies or other professionals have been involved with the child, this information, together with associated written reports, is considered. Observations from parents are also crucially important in establishing quality provision for children.

When a child is first identified as having special educational needs or disabilities (SEND), quality practitioners adopt a positive stance. They inform families that the great majority of children with SEN or disabilities find work, and are able to live independently, and participate in their community.

Quality multi-professional working involves practitioners who are strong communicators. When such an approach is called for, health workers, social workers, early years providers and schools should work closely together. Quality multi-professional teams strive to help children with SEND to achieve the best outcomes in life right from the start.

Conclusion

Policies about quality provision emerge on the landscape at frequent intervals and early years leaders and teams must become familiar with these, and then apply them to their settings with minimal support from outside agencies. This chapter has highlighted some of the key policies relating to quality provision and has invited practitioners to consider how to apply these in their own settings.

References

Dahlberg, G., Moss, P., & Pence, A. (2007). *Beyond quality in early childhood education and care: Languages of evaluation* (2nd ed.). London: Routledge.

Department for Children, Schools and Families. (2008). *Statutory framework for the early years foundation stage.* London: DCSF.

Department for Education. (2011). *The early years: Foundations for life, health and learning - an independent report on the early years foundation stage to Her Majesty's government (the Tickell Review).* London: DfE.

Department for Education. (2012a). *Foundations for quality: The independent review of early education and childcare qualifications (Nutbrown Report).* London: DfE.

Department for Education. (2012b). *Statutory framework for the early years foundation stage.* London: DfE.

Department for Education. (2012c). *Teachers' standards.* London: DfE.

Department for Education. (2013). *Early years outcomes: A non-statutory guide for practitioners and inspectors to help inform understanding of child development through the early years.* London: DfE.

Department for Education. (2014). *Statutory framework for the early years foundation stage.* London: DfE.

Early Education. (2012). *Development matters in the early years foundation stage (EYFS).* British Association for Early Childhood Education/Department for Education (DfE).

Her Majesty's Treasury Office. (2003). *Every child matters.* London: Her Majesty's Stationery Office (HMSO).

Mathers, S., Eisenstadt, N., Sylva, K., Soukakou, E., & Ereky-Stevens, K. (2014). *Sound foundations: A review of the research evidence on quality of early childhood education and care for children under three.* Oxford: Oxford University and The Sutton Trust.

National College for Teaching and Leadership. (2013). *Teachers' standards (early years).* London: National College for Teaching and Leadership and Department for Education.

Office for Standards in Education, Children's Services and Skills. (2015). *Early years inspection handbook.* London: Ofsted.

Osgood, J. (2012). *Narratives from the nursery.* London: Routledge.

Owen, P., & Gillentine, J. (2011). Please touch the children: Appropriate touch in the primary classroom. *Early Child Development and Care, 181*(6), 857–868.

7 Quality education and care for vulnerable children

Isabelle Brodie

The concept of the 'vulnerable child' carries with it particular meaning in the twenty-first century. In the context of children's services, it denotes children whose circumstances are such that additional services may be required. This chapter aims to examine the theoretical, policy and practice context for our current understanding of 'vulnerable children', and what is meant by an appropriate service response within universal services for young children. This includes the identification and assessment of vulnerability, and questions of how best early years professionals can intervene effectively to support children and their families. This is central to both keeping children safe and to promoting their well-being.

These issues are complex, and can be difficult to disentangle in a context where much of the public debate relating to safeguarding focuses on high-profile cases of child death that receive extensive attention from the media. But, of course, a great number of children will still face vulnerabilities and yet will never reach the threshold for statutory safeguarding service; these children will be supported through universal provision; for example, their early years provision. The emphasis on placing 'blame' on individuals in relation to high-profile cases can result in high levels of anxiety among professionals (Ayre, 2001; Munro, 2010; Munro, 2011). If children are to be kept safe, it is important that all professionals recognize an ongoing responsibility for learning and understanding their role in relation to vulnerable children. This entails both statutory responsibilities— responsibilities of the early years professional as an individual and for their setting as set out in law and official government guidance, together with continued learning as a professional in relation to the social, emotional and physical needs of all children.

Vulnerability cannot easily be defined, nor is there a 'blueprint' listing all indicators of vulnerability. It will usually involve a variety of factors that are frequently interlinked, but are not necessarily permanent. It is essential that early years professionals do not associate vulnerability with any single social group or class; and they should not assume that because of the nature of their setting or catchment area, they will or will not encounter vulnerability. All families will experience times of stress and difficulty, and children from all social groups and communities may be vulnerable at times in their lives. That said, poverty, substance misuse, mental health problems and domestic violence represent factors that are likely to create stressful and sometimes dangerous environments for children, and will place them at greater risk of abuse and maltreatment.

Moss and Petrie (2002) comment that the ideas that are held concerning early years care and education should be recognized as reflecting particular values and ideas about the family. These ideas are many and varied. Consequently, the way in which work in this area is approached should not be viewed as inevitable, and it is important to unpick the values that inform practice. Similarly, views about care and protection of vulnerable children and their families have changed dramatically over the past century. This is, in part, due to the development of knowledge concerning children's health and well-being, but it is also linked to our changing views on childhood itself and what constitutes 'good parenting'. To this extent the idea of 'quality' in relation to support for vulnerable children and their families is contested: there are tensions in what is viewed as desirable, and how much and what kind of help is available. The question of what represents positive and 'effective' work with vulnerable children and their families also takes place in a context where the specific role of early years professionals has been under-researched. This relates to the more general neglect of early years services in the UK (Pugh, 1996) and also to a lack of attention to the nature of services to young children, even to those identified as being in need or in care. This chapter begins by considering the meaning of vulnerability in relation to thinking about 'risk' and the wider social conditions in which families live. It goes on to examine the legal and policy framework.

Risk and vulnerability

It is easy to rush to judgement on what makes a child 'vulnerable'. Variously, this may be considered obvious and a matter of common sense, or a matter that can only be decided in relation to individual children (what makes one child vulnerable is not true of others) or as resulting from a universal standard of vulnerability, perhaps defined by legislation or guidance. Each of these judgements depends, in part, on what is considered to place a child at 'risk'. Safeguarding guidance states that 'professionals working in universal services have a responsibility to identify the symptoms and triggers of abuse and neglect, to share that information and work together to provide children and young people with the help they need' (Department for Education, 2015, p. 15). This guidance states that professionals should be especially alert to certain situations; for example, a child who:

- is disabled and has specific additional needs
- has special educational needs (SEN)
- is a young carer
- is showing signs of engaging in antisocial or criminal behaviour

- is in a family circumstance presenting challenges for the child, such as substance abuse, adult mental health problems and domestic violence
- has returned home to their family from care
- is showing early signs of abuse and/or neglect

However, there are problems in simply listing what constitutes risk—the stories of individual families will invariably be more complex and are likely to involve a range of factors. Often, as well, they will include wider social problems that are not easily amenable to the intervention of any service or any professional.

Poverty is the most obvious of these, and is central to the way in which vulnerability is understood, and what makes a child vulnerable. Poverty is not uncommon: there are 3.5 million children, 27 per cent (or just over one in every four) of the entire child population, living in poverty at the present time (Child Poverty Action Group, 2015). It is frequently linked to other issues, so families where an adult member is disabled are more likely to be poor; and families from minority ethnic groups are also more likely to live in poverty. In itself poverty does not cause individuals to neglect or harm their children, but the stresses and difficulties associated with living in poverty can create conditions in which this is more likely. Families who live in poverty are also likely to experience other adversities that may contribute to both their poverty and parenting difficulties; for example, poor housing, lack of access to public services and amenities, mental and physical health difficulties.

Reflection point 7.1

At any one time, therefore, about one quarter of the children in your setting could be considered to be vulnerable. What measures do you have in place to be alert to these vulnerabilities? Is there anything more you can do to further support families and children facing disadvantages?

At your next team meeting, collectively 'map' all the different support services available to families and children in your local area. How might you share this information with parents? This could be as simple as putting posters up from local debt advice or housing services, or you might be able to have a range of leaflets available for parents: most services provide these at no cost.

Understanding the relationship between poverty and vulnerability is essential for early years professionals seeking to support vulnerable children and their families. In achieving this it will be important to understand the communities and wider social networks in which vulnerable families live, and the stresses they may encounter on a day-to-day basis and will, therefore, enable you to support the child's needs and development better. White, Morris, Featherstone, Brendon, and Thoburn (2014), discussing the role of social workers in providing early help and intervention, note that the pressures of social work and the way in which case work has developed has militated against this understanding of the context of poverty. It is frequently what Gupta (2015) calls the 'elephant in the room': the evidence of the association is almost overwhelming, yet political remedies to the problems of safeguarding children focus almost exclusively on professional actions and responses.

In this respect, early years professionals, who will see families on a regular basis and whose settings are located within communities, are very well situated to work effectively with vulnerable children and parents. The early years sector has a powerful history in seeking to alleviate poverty in the broadest sense. Industrialization in Britain in the nineteenth century resulted in large numbers of people moving to the cities from the country in search of work in the new mills and factories. The populations of cities like Glasgow, Manchester and London grew rapidly, but housing and other services did not keep pace and many families were living in overcrowded slum conditions. Poverty, with associated disease and violence, became visible in a way that had not previously been the case. It quickly became clear that existing provision—in the form of parish relief and the workhouse—was not sufficient. This was borne out by the social surveys undertaken by Seebohm Rowntree in York and Charles Booth in London in the late nineteenth century, which highlighted the extreme deprivation of certain communities.

These revelations contributed to changing ideas about childhood, and the need to ensure that children's development and welfare was protected. Hendrick (1997) describes different historical phases in the development of our ideas concerning childhood, and suggests that the late nineteenth century saw the emergence of the 'welfare child', as the state played an increasing role in the lives of children and their families. A national system of schools was established, and new welfare legislation in the early twentieth century introduced medical checks for children. While these developments may be viewed as largely positive, we should also be aware that they were accompanied by growing scrutiny and regulation, especially the families of the poor. Carlen, Gleeson, and Wardhaugh (1992), examining the development of the education welfare service, note that as schools became stricter regarding attendance, so families became more resentful of the intrusion of truancy services into their lives.

This tension between 'protection' and invading the privacy of the private domain of the families continues to be significant in work with vulnerable children today. Hooper, Gorin, Cabral, and Dyson (2007) found that even while encountering significant parenting difficulties and often with their own experiences of abuse and violence, individuals' identity as parents was extremely important: perhaps more so in the context where individual value was not derived from education, work or leisure. Their pride in being parents, together with negative associations regarding social care, presented a challenging set of circumstances for professionals. Families felt very strongly that such intervention was stigmatizing and were often extremely hostile to the idea of working with professionals. In this respect, evidence attesting to the insensitive nature of service intervention, and the way in which this is embedded in the histories of communities is important (McKenzie, 2014). This may be associated with other forms of discrimination, including racism.

Reflection point 7.2

Within early years we recognize the importance of working in partnership with parents and valuing parents as the child's first and most important educator. Almost all settings have a 'parental involvement policy' and all are required to have a safeguarding children policy. Look at these policies side by side.

- Are there any contradictions between the two or do they truly support one another?

- Try to consider the policies from a parent's perspective, given the above, are there any changes you might like to make?

The policy and legislative framework

Acknowledging social disadvantage is crucial to understanding the way in which vulnerability may arise. However, it is also essential to understand the system through which the state intervenes to protect vulnerable children. The primary legislation relating to the safety and protection of children in England and Wales is the Children Act of 1989 (Great Britain, 1989, Section 17). Parallel legislation embodying the same principles exists in Scotland and Northern Ireland. Within this legislation 'children' are defined as any child or young person under 18 years old.

Underpinning the Act is the view that decisions concerning children should always have the child at their centre. The welfare of the child is paramount. The Act, therefore, holds a holistic view of the care of children and emphasizes the need to consider all aspects of a child's development; for example. their health, education and cultural and religious needs. Following from this, professionals from different services will need to work together in order to meet a child's needs. The voice of children themselves is also crucial, as the Act requires that children, according to their age and understanding, should be consulted in decisions affecting them.

The Children Act 1989 also represented a significant departure from previous legislation in arguing that, where possible, the removal of children from their parents should be avoided, unless the safety and welfare of the child is at immediate risk. Instead, this legislation emphasizes the need for professionals to work in partnership with parents, and where possible to support children at home with their parents. To this end the Act introduced a new category of 'children in need':

A child is in need if:

- he or she is unlikely to achieve or maintain a reasonable standard of health or development without the provision of services from the local authority

- his or her health or development is likely to be significantly impaired, or further improved, without the provision of services from the local authority

- he or she is disabled. (Great Britain, 1989, Section 17)

Reflection point 7.3

Consider in detail the above definition. Does this fit with your own thoughts on what might define a child 'in need'? When considering your own definition you might have considered phrases such as 'at risk of not achieving their full potential' but here the definition talks only of a 'reasonable' standard of health or development.

The principles of the Children Act 1989 have been reinforced by subsequent legislation, notably the Children Act 2004 (Great Britain, 2004). This reinforced the importance of addressing the holistic needs of the child as set out in the *Every child matters* framework (Her Majesty's Treasury, 2003). These proposed five outcomes are: 'be healthy'; 'stay safe'; 'enjoy and achieve'; 'make a positive contribution'; and 'achieve economic well-being'. These outcomes were applied to assessment and decision making for individual children, and, while no longer representing current policy, continue to influence much professional thinking.

Few people would disagree with the principles of the Children Act legislation. Inevitably, however, there is a gap between the vision of the legislation and what happens in practice, and there are specific issues associated with the application of these principles in the context of early years practice. At a policy level there have been tensions between the welfare-driven approach of the Children Acts and more recent policy relating specifically to early years. The absence of a co-ordinated approach to the development of early years services, and an educational focus on curriculum and testing as opposed to well-being, can impede the partnership approach necessary to support vulnerable children and their families.

Since the implementation of the Children Act 1989, there have been ongoing debates regarding the best way to protect and safeguard children. During the 1990s a series of research studies emerged which argued that too much emphasis was still being placed on 'high-end' child abuse cases, with services focusing on investigation; preventative services were being neglected and lacked investment

(Department of Health, 1995). Models of work that incorporated both parents and children were also poorly developed (Tunstill, 1995) and there was a lack of understanding of the specific needs of vulnerable children and families from minority ethnic groups (Qureshi, Berridge, & Wenman, 2000; Thoburn, Chand, & Procter, 2005).

Prevention and early intervention

According to the Department of Health (1995, p.55):

> A more balanced service for vulnerable children would encourage professionals to take a wider view. There would be efforts to work alongside families rather than disempower them, to raise their self-esteem rather than reproach families, to promote family relationships where children have their needs met, rather than leave untreated families with an unsatisfactory parenting style.

Since this Department of Health document was written, there has been a growing interest and recognition at policy level of the importance of early help to prevent the development of more serious family problems. Research reviews have emphasized the importance of intervention that is early in the sense of identifying problems before they become more serious, as well as early in a child's life. This concern has been reflected in high-profile reviews of early intervention, most notably the Allen Review (2011). Preventing problems from escalating seems a matter of common sense, but the evidence indicates that, more importantly, a preventative model can keep a greater number of children safe. The Munro Review (2011) into child protection has argued convincingly that a change needs to be made from an approach that is reactive to one that is proactive.

Examination of the research, however, indicates that there are different ways of thinking about early help and intervention, and how this help should be delivered. Key questions include:

- How are the problems of children and families requiring early help to be explained? Are these problems attributable to the characteristics of the individual child (for example, patterns of brain development) or should the focus be on wider social issues, such as poverty and associated problems such as poor housing?
- Should early help be delivered in the context of universal (that is, services for everyone such as health and education) or should they be targeted at those who are identified as most vulnerable? If the decision is made to provide universal services, how can we ensure that those who are most in need access those services? If the decision is made to focus on the most vulnerable, how are these children and families identified?

- Following from these questions, what are the roles and responsibilities of the different services working with children and families? What kind of specialist knowledge and professional skills need to be available?

These are complex and controversial issues. The vignette below is an example of the different ways in which these questions become visible in individual cases. Then, after reading it, consider the key questions in relation to Joshua and Szymon and their families.

Vignette: Joshua

Joshua is 3 years old and has just been attending Southwood Children's Centre for six weeks. He is known to children's social care services. His mother, Dani, has been in a physically abusive relationship with Joshua's father, JJ, for four years and there have been several incidents in which the police have been involved. Dani also smokes, uses cannabis regularly and has a record of binge drinking. She tried to stop all of these while pregnant with Joshua but her health visitor is fairly sure she did not manage this. She has moved between dependence on benefits to earning money through dealing in cannabis, for which she has been arrested. She has a difficult relationship with her mother and appears to lack any support network. Joshua presents at the Children's Centre as a very anxious and volatile child. He regularly kicks and bites other children, and tears up his own and other children's work into tiny pieces. He refuses to sit on a chair but curls up as far away from the other children as possible. He has also tried to run away three times.

Joshua's key worker, Alice, has been very concerned from the outset. She tried to make a home visit before Joshua started at nursery, but when she went to the house no one answered—though she is sure someone was in. Dani has either laughed off her concerns or, most recently, told Alice in no uncertain terms that she did not need to be told how to look after her son. Joshua has not turned up to nursery for the past week. Several of Alice's colleagues have commented 'Thank goodness' or 'Let's hope he stays away for a bit'.

Vignette: Szymon

Alice is also a key worker for Szymon whose family have recently arrived from Poland. Initially, Szymon's father, Joachim, was working as a labourer on a construction site, but has been injured and can no longer work. His mother, Marya, is finding adjustment to life in the UK very difficult. Alice suspects she is depressed. Szymon is proving a challenging child. The only activity he will take part in is building a tower from coloured bricks. This is done repetitively for long periods of time, and he is resistant to any interaction with staff. The family have no income and, despite efforts by the Children's Centre, do not seem to be connecting with the local Polish community. Alice is anxious as she thinks Szymon may have SEN. She has tried to talk to both parents but they seem embarrassed and ashamed.

Reflection point 7.4

- How would you describe Joshua and Syzmon's problems?
- Do you think early years services should intervene? Why?
- What could you do in the setting to support Joshua and Syzmon?
- What kind of services do you think are needed? What might your role be in supporting parents to access these services?

Government initiatives in recent decades have adopted different perspectives on questions such as these, but they have been present throughout history. Rowbotham (2010) provides a fascinating insight into how ideas about the welfare of children fused with early feminism: individuals worked with women in communities, and crèches and nurseries were often part of this. There was, therefore, a strong association between helping women into work and the provision of quality childcare. This tended to be concentrated in poor neighbourhoods, as wealthier women either stayed at home to look after their children or employed servants to do so. Work with poor families to alleviate poverty and support their parenting was considered emancipatory in that it enabled women to learn new skills. At the same time, the recurrent nature of such intervention as oriented to women and with negative connotations of judgements about the quality of their mothering can act as a barrier to working in partnership with parents, who may view the experience as judgemental.

The most significant in recent years has been the Sure Start initiative, developed under the New Labour Government. Sure Start Local Programmes (SSLPs) were established from 2000 onwards. By 2004 524 SSLPs were in existence and working with one-third of all children under 4 years old. Sure Start represents an important turning point in thinking about working with vulnerable families and safeguarding in the early years sector. It aimed to address the cycle of intergenerational social exclusion that 'happens when people or places suffer from a series of problems such as unemployment, discrimination, poor skills, low incomes, poor housing, high crime, ill health and family breakdown' (Office of the Deputy Prime Minister, 2004, p. 1). This interconnection meant that the issues experienced by vulnerable children and families had to be addressed holistically, with a range of services working in partnership. Although the organization of SSLPs varies, all had to demonstrate this partnership approach and in many programmes this was physically manifest, with different professionals working from a single base. It was also considered essential that programmes should work with parents or carers and children, and that services should be universal; that is, available to everyone in the designated Sure Start area.

Criticisms of the Sure Start approach have drawn attention to both the underpinning assumptions of the model and the ways in which it was implemented (Clark, 2006; Tunstill, Allnock, Akhurst, & Garbers, 2005). Tunstill and colleagues note that, in terms of the protection of children, the partnership approach of SSLPs was frequently flawed, with uneven knowledge among professionals of how to work with the complex needs of vulnerable children and their families. The evaluation of the Sure Start initiative was complex and, arguably, flawed by virtue of the local design of Sure Start programmes but the findings from the national evaluation were mixed and did not indicate that the new model of working had a significant effect on most outcomes for children and families (Rutter, 2007). There are many possible explanations for the lack of impact, and there is a considerable amount of qualitative evidence attesting to positive outcomes for individual children and families who received Sure Start services, but inevitably questions were raised about the effectiveness of the model.

From 2004 Sure Start centres became 'Children's Centres', building on the foundation that Sure Start had established, but with some differences in approach. Specifically, a shift was made from the universal to the increasingly targeted (Lewis, 2010) with some Children's Centres in more affluent areas offering only information services. Statutory guidance describes their core purpose as being to provide services for families with young children in their areas, and to reduce inequalities between them. Their focus is on improving outcomes for children, and especially those in greatest need. This targeted approach also fits with other trends in children's services more generally, specifically in early years—notably the focus on parenting programmes and the 'Troubled Families' initiative.

What is known about effective early help?

Much of the work undertaken by Sure Start and Children's Centres was characterized by many of the features that are known to be associated with good practice, and especially the importance of early help. This continues to be very important in guidance relating to support for vulnerable children and families. In order for such help to be provided, the child and family will need to be assessed using an assessment tool such as the Common Assessment Framework (CAF) (Department for Education, 2015). This assessment should take place with the consent of the family, and involves the appointment of a 'lead professional' who co-ordinates the gathering of information and meetings where the findings from the assessment can be discussed. This may be the task of an early years professional, depending on the network of services involved with the family.

An overview of research into vulnerable children (Sharp & Filmer-Sankey, 2010) summarizes these tasks as follows:

- addressing structural disadvantages such as poverty, poor health and low educational achievement among parents/carers
- providing interventions aimed at meeting the needs of adults and children simultaneously and tackling multiple sources of stress within the family
- providing opportunities for parents to develop their basic skills; for example, in literacy and numeracy
- developing parenting skills, especially for young parents and parents of children with behavioural problems
- supporting looked-after children, especially their learning, mental health and accommodation needs

The value of early help and the characteristics of good practice listed above appear eminently sensible, but do not capture the challenges of this area of work—'addressing structural disadvantage' is not easy, and is likely to involve engagement with, for example, housing and benefit systems. The experiences of parents and other family members may also raise issues in terms of what kind of intervention is considered acceptable. White et al. (2014) emphasize that rather than seeking quick results, time is required to build relationships. Work with vulnerable families is stressful and demanding, and it is essential that the workers involved receive sufficient support.

Reflection point 7.5

Already we have read about a wide variety of research, policy and government initiatives relating to early years. As a practitioner within the field, how can you ensure you keep fully up to date and informed of new developments affecting your profession? Discuss with others how they ensure they are kept up to date—what websites, newsfeeds, and so on do they subscribe to?

Then, think about how you can ensure you effectively share what information you receive and what the implications for practice are. This is all part of being a quality professional.

Eileen Munro's review of safeguarding practice in the UK draws attention to characteristics of social work, which may be applied to work with vulnerable children more generally. She emphasizes the complexity of such work, and the need for appropriate skills and training. In order to protect children effectively, professionals will need to be able to ask difficult questions and to persevere in situations where parents are reluctant to engage.

There is a chain of thinking here that requires disentangling. Asking difficult questions will require the individual practitioner to be aware of their role as a professional, who has a legal, professional and moral responsibility for the safety and welfare of the child. This awareness needs to translate into sufficient confidence to ask questions and talk to colleagues and/or other professionals in order to understand the child's needs. The early years practitioner should be supported in this by their line manager and by other agencies, but it should be acknowledged that this support is not, unfortunately, always available. Where this is the case, then it is essential that the early years professional retains a focus on the welfare of the child and ensures that concerns are, where deemed necessary, referred to children's social care services.

The Scottish Government has identified five questions any practitioner should ask when faced with a concern about a child:

- What is getting in the way of this child's well-being?
- Do I have all the information I need to help the child?
- What can I do now to help this child?
- What can my agency do to help this child?
- What additional help, if any, may be needed from others? (Scottish Government, 2015)

If the practitioner has concerns about the safety of the child, then four further critical questions should be asked:

- Why do I think this child is not safe?
- What is getting in the way of this child being safe?
- What have I observed, heard or identified from the child's history that causes concern?
- Are there factors that indicate risk of significant harm present, and, in my view, is the severity of factors enough to warrant immediate action?

In order to provide appropriate support, it will be important for practitioners to understand the nature of current policies and procedures that provide a framework for practice. Where further information and training about these issues is required, the most obvious and immediate source of information will be the practitioner's Local Safeguarding Children's Board in England and Wales, or Child Protection Committee in Scotland.

After initial enquiries have been made, there are a number of options available. This is important as early years professionals need to be aware that a referral and investigation does not mean that a child will be removed from their family. Rather, this process should support the provision of additional services where these are needed. The possible options are:

- no further child protection action, though it may be decided that the child and family would benefit from additional input; for example, help with parenting
- further support is needed from children's services, and designation as a child in need
- the view that a child is at risk of significant harm is confirmed and a strategy discussion takes place, involving all relevant professionals, the family and the child. If this discussion indicates that there is indeed significant harm, then a 'Section 47' enquiry will take place
- it is agreed that a Section 47 enquiry is required. This involves a detailed assessment of the child's welfare and safety needs. A case conference will also take place, involving the different professionals who are working with the child and family

If a child is identified as being at immediate risk, then the children's services child protection team or the police should be contacted immediately. If there is risk of immediate harm, the case will be taken to the courts for a decision on what should happen to the child

---

Reflection point 7.6

Next time you have emerging concerns about a child, use the first five questions as the basis for a discussion with a manager or the nominated person for safeguarding in your setting. You will notice that the question of what you can do to help the child comes before the question of what additional help is required from others.

Remember that the CAF allows for the person with responsibility for intervention to be an early years professional (just as the 'named person' in Scotland can be). This means that rather than your 'passing on' concern for someone else to act upon, you will be expected to draw on the support of others; but it is likely that, in the majority of cases that do not require immediate action, documenting and addressing the child's additional needs and vulnerabilities will remain firmly with the early years setting which they attend.

Young children who are looked after

A small proportion of children will not be able to remain with their families and will become 'looked after' or 'in care'. Under the Children Act 1989 there are two legal options. Section 20 of the Act provides the option for children to be 'looked after' or to enter care on a voluntary basis. Section 31 of the Act provides compulsory options, or orders made by the courts. The language can be confusing and is often used interchangeably.

The Department for Education (DfE) publishes annual statistics relating to children in care. In 2014 there were 15 320 children of 0–4 years old in the care system in England (around one-quarter of the total), primarily for reasons of 'abuse and neglect' and 'family dysfunction' (Department for Education, 2014). These numbers are not large; the distribution of such children is uneven, and it is possible that early years professionals may only rarely encounter a child who is looked after. In this context it is important that professionals know where they can obtain information and support about their responsibilities.

It is also important to emphasize, though, that entry into care may not be permanent and children may move in and out of the care system. In an important piece of research, Ward, Brown, and Maskell-Graham (2012) tracked a group of 57 children who were identified as being at risk of significant harm at 1 years old. By 3 years old, 43 children remained in the sample. Of these, approximately one-third were still living at home, with their parents having overcome the difficulties that had led to referral to social care in the first place; another one-third were living at home but the difficulties remained; and a remaining one-third of the children had been permanently separated and were living in care. However, the researchers concluded that two of the children who had been placed in care had suffered the 'double jeopardy' of having had their initial care placements and their attachment to carers disrupted before a more permanent placement was found. Other children in the sample experienced a 'yo-yo' effect of a series of care episodes interspersed with returns home. In this context staff in early years settings often felt they were providing essential stability in children's lives, but expressed frustration that better planning and decision making had not taken place.

Children who are looked after are not, therefore, a discrete and segregated group. However, the role and nature of the care system are often misunderstood, in part, as a result of the largely negative media commentary relating to care, which rarely considers the experiences of young children. It is important that early years professionals do not carry assumptions about what is 'good' or 'bad' about the care system, and should recognize that there is positive evidence about outcomes for children who experience longer-term support within the care system. At the same time, it should be recognized that children usually enter care because they have experienced serious problems, including abuse, at home. This may be significant in terms of their later behaviour. For older children, educational outcomes are often significantly below those of their non-looked-after peers (Brodie & Morris, 2010). Considerable progress has been made in terms of measurable outcomes for younger children, and recent statistics indicate that at Key Stages 1 and 2 the attainment gap between looked-after and non-looked-after children is closing. Nevertheless, looked-after children of all ages present high levels of special educational need, and are more likely to experience mental health problems.

Young children who enter care will live either with foster carers or with other members of their extended families, known as 'family and friends' placements. Almost no residential care is now provided for young children in the UK, though it remains widespread internationally. Clearly, early years practitioners may be involved at all stages of the child's entry into care, including identification of the abuse and alerting police and other authorities. However, it is also important that consideration is given to the role of practitioners once the child is living in a placement. These will include:

- Continued attention to the child's development and well-being, including listening to the child itself. Relatively little research has been undertaken to elicit the views of young children in care, but Winter (2010) undertook 10 case studies involving individual interviews with young children 4–7 years old in care. The children in the study had strong memories of the abuse and neglect they had experienced. Winter found that the children wanted to talk about their experiences, and suggests that there had been an absence of 'safe spaces' where they were able to discuss their experiences. More than that, many children felt they had not been listened to.

- On a day-to-day basis, communicating with carers to provide updates on a child's well-being and developmental progress, even if this is made more difficult by the vulnerabilities of the child and the circumstances at the time. This may also involve responding to requests from foster carers for advice and information. If a placement is to endure, then good information about the child is essential. Practitioners will need to work with carers to ensure they are working consistently in relation to any difficulties a child may have. The early years practitioner may be the remaining trusted individual for the child, and it is essential that they are sensitive to the trauma they have experienced in being separated from the family.

- Participating in care planning and other meetings to provide written and verbal updates on the child's development and well-being. Again, this will involve thought being given to how to take account of children's views and experiences. Practitioners will also need to work with social care colleagues and carers to produce personal education plans and to record progress appropriately.

Conclusion

Maintaining a strong dialogue with parents, enabling children the opportunity to access safe spaces to talk, and a willingness and commitment to working in partnership with others involved in supporting the child and their family, are not practices that should be reserved only for those who face immediate vulnerabilities. Instead, they form a basis for quality practice with all children, not least because a child's situation can change dramatically and suddenly (through family breakdown, a sudden bereavement or a move to a new home) but also because by practising in such a way will also work towards reducing the risk and vulnerability of those already identified as being 'at risk' as well as those on the verge of. It is this early intervention and preventative approach to working that will have the greatest impact on reducing the number of children whose lives are adversely affected by preventable vulnerabilities. Early years providers are key to achieving this, but it takes a collaborative approach.

References

Allen, G. (2011). *Early intervention: The next steps*. London: Department for Education (DfE).

Ayre, P. (2001). Child protection and the media: Lessons from the last three decades. *British Journal of Social Work, 31*(6), 887–901.

Brodie, I., & Morris, M. (2010). *Improving the educational outcomes of looked after children and young people*. London: Centre for Excellence and Outcomes in Children and Young People's Services.

Carlen, P., Gleeson, D., & Wardhaugh, J. (1992). *Truancy: The politics of compulsory schooling*. Maidenhead: Open University Press.

Child Poverty Action Group. (2015). *Child poverty: Facts and figures*. Retrieved from http://www.cpag.org.uk/child-poverty-facts-and-figures

Clark, K. (2006). Childhood, parenting and early intervention: A critical examination of the Sure Start national programme. *Critical Social Policy, 26*(4), 699–721.

Department for Education. (2014). *Statistical first release: Children looked after in England 2014 (including adoption and care leavers) year ending 31 March 2014 (SFR 36/2014)*. London: Department for Education (DfE).

Department for Education. (2015). *Working together to safeguard children*. London: Department for Education (DfE).

Department of Health. (1995). *Child protection: Messages from research*. London: Her Majesty's Stationery Office (HMSO).

Great Britain. (1989). *Children Act, 1989: Elizabeth II c41*. London: Her Majesty's Stationery Office (HMSO).

Great Britain. (2004). *Children Act, 2004: Elizabeth II c31*. London: Her Majesty's Stationery Office (HMSO).

Gupta, A. (2015). *Poverty and child neglect—the elephant in the room?* Bristol: Policy Press.

Hendrick, H. (1997). *Children, childhood and English society, 1880–1990*. Cambridge: Cambridge University Press.

Her Majesty's Treasury. (2003). *Every child matters*. London: Her Majesty's Stationery Office (HMSO).

Hooper, C. A., Gorin, S., Cabral, C., & Dyson, C. (2007). *Living with hardship 24/7: The diverse experiences of families living in poverty in England*. London: The Frank Buttle Trust.

Lewis, J. (2010). From Sure Start to children's centres: An analysis of policy change in English early years programmes. *Journal of Social Policy, 40*(1), 71–88.

McKenzie, L. (2014). *Estates, class and culture in austerity Britain*. London: Policy Press.

Moss, P., & Petrie, P. (2002). *From children's services to children's spaces: Public policy, children and childhood*. London: Routledge.

Munro, E. (2011). *The Munro Review of Child Protection Part 1: A systems analysis*. London: Department for Education (DfE).

Munro, E. (2010). Learning to reduce risk in child protection. *The British Journal of Social Work, 40*(4), 1135–1151.

Office of the Deputy Prime Minister. (2004) *The social inclusion unit*. London: Cabinet Office.

Pugh, G. (Ed.). (1996). *Contemporary issues in the early years*. London: National Children's Bureau.

Qureshi, T., Berridge, D., & Wenman, H. (2000). *Where to Turn? Family support for South Asian families*. York: Joseph Rowntree Foundation.

Rowbotham, S. (2010). *Dreamers of a new day*. London: Verso.

Rutter, M. (2007). Is Sure Start an effective preventive intervention? *Child and Adolescent Mental Health, 11*(3), 135–141.

Scottish Government. (2015). P*ractice Briefing 1: The role of the Named Person*. Retrieved from http://www.gov.scot/Resource/Doc/1141/0109328.pdf

Sharp, C., & Filmer-Sankey, C. (2010). *Early intervention and prevention in the context of integrated services: Evidence from C4EO and Narrowing the Gap Reviews*. London: Centre for Excellence and Outcomes in Children and Young People's Services.

Thoburn, J., Chand, A., & Procter, J. (2005). *Child welfare services for minority ethnic families: The research reviewed*. London: Jessica Kingsley.

Tunstill, J. (1995). The concept of children in need: The answer or the problem for family support? *Children and Youth Services Review, 17*(5/6), 651–667.

Tunstill, J., Allnock, D., Akhurst, S., & Garbers, C. (2005). Sure Start Local Programmes: Implications of case study data from the National Evaluation of Sure Start. *Children and Society, 19*(2), 158–171.

Ward, H., Brown, R., & Maskell-Graham, D. (2012). *Young children suffering, or likely to suffer, significant harm: Experiences on entering education (Research Report DfE-RR209)*. London: Department for Education (DfE).

White, S., Morris, K., Featherstone, B., Brendon, M., & Thoburn, J. (2014). Re-imagining early help: looking forward, looking back. In M. Blyth (Ed.), *Moving on from Munro: Improving children's services* (pp. 73–88). Bristol: Policy Press.

Winter, K. (2010). The perspectives of young children in care. *Child and Family Social Work, 15*, 186–195.

8   Quality early years professionals
Emma Slaughter

Introduction

This chapter invites you to explore the notion of the early years 'professional'—what one is, or might be, and the influences at play in its construction. A consideration of both tacit and explicit inferences within politically endorsed agendas relating to notions of 'the professional' in early years will form a backdrop to your exploration, from which you will be provoked to consider your own notions of what constitutes a 'quality early years professional', given what you have identified as being important for quality practice thus far, particularly from Chapter 1.

Reflection point 8.1

Before you move on, you are invited to make a list of the characteristics, attributes, skills and behaviours that you associate with a 'quality professional'. Then, for each aspect, make notes on 'why' you feel each of them to be important. Put the list to one side; you will be returning to it later in the chapter.

The changing face of the professional identity in early years

The Government's Workforce Strategy (Department for Education and Skills) (DfES) introduced in 2006 set out the government's agenda for developing the early years workforce. This, alongside the consultation of the Early Years Foundation Stage (EYFS) placed practitioners at the heart of the reform agenda that was to follow, with skills, confidence and competences framing this 'increased' professionalism. On one hand, this transformation agenda required a greater degree of reflectiveness to professionals' practice, which implied a requirement for a greater degree of creativity, independence and, undoubtedly, responsibility, to those working in the field of early years. These softer attributes have a 'personal' feel about them and so infer that professionalism is an 'individually rooted' paradigm. And yet, 2008 saw the introduction of the EYFS (Department for Education and Skills, 2008) that presented—what might be considered to be—a more prescriptive legislative curriculum framework for practitioners to work within. Framing all of this was tighter government control and regulation through a revised registration and inspection processes from Office for Standards in Education, Children's Services and Skills (Ofsted). Dissonance was thus created whereby early years professionals faced an externally originated drive to be independent, creative, reflective and self-developing and highly qualified—ultimately more highly regarded, perhaps—and yet the context that now enveloped them contradicted that by imposing tighter regulatory control and scrutiny. Oberheumer (2005) explores this dissonance through her concept of 'democratic professionalism'—quality practice within an increasingly regulated and controlled professional context.

So far in this book we have only really touched on political changes affecting the field of early years and we shall explore them in more detail here. There is much speculation around how these political changes affect the immediate and longer-term service provision for young children, many of whom are vulnerable. However, there is very little reference to be found about how this alters or influences more broader constructs of those working within the field—not least the question of just who or what is 'the early years professional' and how has their role changed in recent years? Given that we currently live and operate in austere times, where efficiency, performance-orientation, adaptability and target-meeting are rapidly becoming 'the norm', this shall be considered in terms of how it shapes the ideas of not just what an early years professional is, but what their role is, too. This is important not just for those about to embark on a profession within the field but also for those who entered the field some years ago—the landscape has changed, is changing still, and will continue to change.

Austerity, but at what cost?

To provide a contextual backdrop for considerations of how ideas of the 'professional' in early years are arrived at, it is important to recognize the effects of recent political austerity measures and how they influence how 'professionalism' within the field of early years is enacted, particularly in the public sector and services overseen by it (such as early years care and education). It is important to do so because it provides not only a richer backdrop and understanding of the political context and influences on the sector but also because early years is politically influenced both in terms of inspection and judgement of quality and its resulting construction of societal expectations. We use the term 'austerity measures' in this section to refer to the recent political agenda, brought about initially by the coalition government of 2011 and continued by the current Conservative Government, of dismantling public services through financial reductions to local authorities and allied services and a general drive to 'outsourcing' provisions and services that had traditionally been offered from within the public sector.

Very few publications have considered the effect of such austerity measures on achievement of public services beyond the immediate financial effects; indeed, why would they? They were a relatively recent phenomenon, only really coming to the forefront in 2011. Banks (2013, pp. 5–23) started out by highlighting the effect such austerity measures would have on social work, and raised concern at the increased drive to achieve measurable outputs, reach targets and demonstrate cost effectiveness in the face of sharp financial cuts to such services. Even further than simply raising concerns, Banks went on to suggest that this 'new public management' approach was, in fact, set to adversely affect the ethical practices of similar such professions such as early years as we consider here. Using conduct, behaviour, character and relationships as the four cornerstones of what constitutes 'ethical practice', she raised specific concern that a focus on procedures, targets and evidencing outputs through the new modernization of publicly led (or governed) services, alongside budget cuts, was detrimental to the creativity and efficiency of those who work within those professions and, therefore, highly likely to have significant negative effects on the quality of service being provided. This is particularly relevant to the field of early years because it has, in recent years, gone from being perceived by society as being predominantly a 'care'-based field, with a relatively low degree of scrutiny and recognition, to a much more 'target-driven' field with increased (and further increasing) scrutiny, inspection, performance orientation and expectations (early learning outcomes, 2-year-old checks, school readiness agendas, and so on). For professionals working within the field, therefore, while many may prefer and are capable of creativity, self-direction, autonomy, they are instead somewhat constrained by statutory frameworks for the curriculum they must deliver. Furthermore, they have performance measures detailing where they must move a child's development towards and whereby the very 'quality' of what they deliver is judged by nationally set output- and outcome-focused measures. All of these latter points serve to deplete the foundations of what is surely required to deliver high-quality practice with very young, often vulnerable, children.

Banks (2013) goes on to write about public austerity and the creative tension that is being caused as a result among caring professions as a whole. She considers what the motivations are for staff engaged in such professions, and although not top of the list, a desire to have a job and to earn a living is cited—and in times of austerity it is only natural that many may feel this is compromised. Furthermore, and more importantly in terms of the creation of the professional identity in early years, she goes on to write about how those working in children's services often hold a desire to do more than simply 'follow a set of rules or guidelines'—instead holding a desire to be creative and 'do whatever it takes' to achieve a positive outcome for those they are engaged; the 'sine qua non' or accountability that these professionals feel for their work—feeling responsible personally for the service users' outcomes. And so, instead, a professional desire to 'comply' overrides the personal desire to 'do what is right'.

This was a situation warned against by the Munro Report, which specifically stated that 'for some, following rules and being compliant can appear less risky than carrying the personal responsibility for exercising judgement' (Munroe, 2011, p. 5). Given this, it gives rise to consideration of the emotional impact that early years work has on individual perceptions of professionalism, and to do so alongside questions about the 'personal strive' of wishing to do what is felt 'right' and effective, and yet being constrained in doing so by the subsequent effects of austerity measures. In considering these aspects we begin to understand how professional action and behaviours might be in contrast to personal values and beliefs—and the dissonance that this may bring about to an individual's sense of identity. Thus, we begin to consider the stark reality of how politically driven agendas—not necessarily brought about by 'early years experts'—have a direct impact on what is considered to be 'right' for children and how this shapes and influences the direct practice that takes place in the setting. Furthermore, it shows its influence on how it serves to shape the professional identity of those undertaking this important work. We shall explore this before further moving on.

Early years settings may take a range of forms, from privately run day-care provisions and childminding services to voluntarily led local preschools and play groups. While the desire to 'make a profit' may never have ever been in the initial business design, the fact remains that they need to at least generate adequate income to cover their basic expenditure. Even a setting founded on a charitable structure will need to at least meet its costs. What makes new managerialism 'new' is the much firmer deployment of managerialism principles in both public sector bodies and those that fall under their 'umbrellas'; that is, early years (Lynch, Grummel, & Devine, 2012, p. 12). As referred to earlier, the focus in public sector fields in recent years has been on creating efficiencies and ensuring that services are productive—as measured by government-imposed performance measures and targets (EYFS profile, good levels of development, school readiness, 2-year-old checks, and so on). These notions associated with new managerialism focus the organization and, therefore, the professionals within them on targets. These targets are utilized to measure, monitor or review their progress (Arnaboldi, Lapsley, & Steccolini, 2015, p. 1). It is the success of meeting these objectives, which has now become these organizations', and by default, the professionals', priority as the indicator and measure of whether they are delivering a quality service (Arnaboldi & Lapsley, 2008, pp. 13). It would appear at this stage, therefore, that it is government policy that sets the definition of what constitutes 'quality in early years' through a series of quantitative targets? Does this match with what you as a trained professional in the field (or about to embark on the field), identified in Chapter 1, about what you considered quality provision to be, based on your heightened understanding and knowledge of child development and young children's learning in general? Probably not. If you return to the list you made within the very first refection point of this chapter asking you what you felt the characteristics, attributes and behaviours of an early years professional were, did you list things likes 'judges children's attainment by comparing to others, or routinely measures children's progress against nationally set 'norms'? Again, probably not.

Thus, when the effects of new managerialism are considered, it is possible to assert that these have changed the faces of the role of early years professionals in a number of ways that may impact on practice and pedagogy in the setting (Ahlbäck, Öberg,& Bringselius, 2014, pp. 2–4). First, the notion that all objectives are associated with targets and that these take priority other considerations has changed the way in which people (in this case, children and their families) are seen and the things that they must consider; that is, the learning priorities. For example, there is an increased emphasis on making sure that children achieve as 'expected' levels of development, as deemed by the EYFS (Department for Education and Skills, 2014) and that settings ensure children are 'ready for school' through the delivery of provision that is deemed to be 'good' or 'outstanding' as defined by Ofsted inspection descriptors. Therefore, there has been a fundamental shift in professional culture, which influences the very notion of what a 'good quality professional in early years actually is. Instead of being able to lead practice from a foundation of what is understood to be 'right' for the child in terms of child development, play-based and child-centered learning, there is a much stronger emphasis on doing so within a framework of the focus to be 'Ofsted compliant' and ensuring children meet nationally set targets and levels of development. Undoubtedly this has the very likely potential to influence behaviours and practice in the setting.

Therefore, new managerialism is recognized as a form of political governance that has some control or influence over notions of professionalism within the early years workplace. Where an increased focus is placed on attainments, efficiencies or effectiveness above more broadly-based moral and social values related to care, autonomy, tolerance, respect, trust and equality it shakes the foundations that the whole profession is based on, and the very reason why many go into that field of work in the first place.

You will have already explored in earlier chapters the introduction of Early Years Professional Status (EYPS) (Children Workforce Development Council, 2008), which signalled a move towards an attempt to specify what a 'quality professional was' in terms of their attributes, characteristics and competences. The defined set of national standards supported the idea that an early years professional was something that could be achieved and measured by a predetermined set of descriptors—in essence, a recipe for quality.

Before embarking on reflections about just what a quality early years professional is, however, there are some pertinent points to consider. First, the overwhelming majority of under 5-year-olds access their early years provision within the private, voluntary and independent sector rather than the maintained sector

(Oberhuemer, Schreyer, & Newman, 2010, p. 459). Government initiatives to move young children into school at an earlier age serves to repeal this trend; however, the fact remains that the majority attend provision in the private, voluntary and independent sector and for the very youngest children this is unlikely to be a trend that alters in coming years. Second, since 1997 the UK government's ongoing attempt to integrate early childhood services has been 'dramatically stepped up' (Pugh, 2010, p. 6). This was further motioned by the moving of all early education services into the Department for Education (DfE) around that same time. *Every child matters* in 2004 (Department for Education and Skills , 2004) and the swiftly following Childcare Act in 2006 (Department for Education and Skills, 2006a) reinforced the drive to a more collaborative approach to multi-agency early years working than had ever been seen before. EYPS came to the forefront of this in 2011 when Allen (2011) recommended that all early years settings should employ someone with this 'professional status'. The CWDC at the time cited EYPS as being the 'gold standard' for professionals working with children under 5 years old. The Nutbrown Review, *Foundations for quality* (Department for Education, 2012), and the resulting *More great childcare* report (Department for Education and Skills, 2013) signalled a changed from an early years 'professional status' to early years 'teacher status'. The suggestion from Liz Truss (Children and Families Minister at the time) was that the title of 'teacher' was better understood by parents and representative of the professional role that early years practitioners undertook; an inference perhaps that 'professionalism' came with a name or a job title. This presents an example of inference through policy and political positioning not only that 'professionalism' can be defined but also that through enacting this defined professionalism (which was quantified by a set of 39 competence indicators/ standards but was later reduced to 8), this was the key vehicle for achieving a 'world-class transformational early years sector' (Department for Education and Skills , 2006a). In recent years the UK government has been influential in leading the privatization of early education services (hence the significant proportion of children that are cared for and educated in the private, voluntary and independent sector) and yet this has been counteracted with such a strong political directive of what the market should look like and how it should behave. We further experience by such actions that 'professionalism' can be reduced to a 'series of [39] competencies' (Osgood, 2011, p. 112).

To broaden your reflections, you are asked to consider for a moment how this assumption might sit with those working in the field of early years at the current time of the changes. To do so, you will need to consider the characteristics of different individuals you are likely to find working in early years settings today. The following vignettes outline three 'stereotypical' practitioners and the reflection point that follows will ask you to consider this particular government early years initiative through its lens. If you are based within an early years setting, or have access to early years professionals or teachers, you may wish to ask them about their views instead.

Vignettes: Early years professionals

Anjum is 37 years old and is working part time at a local preschool. She started as a parent helper 10 years ago when her own children were attending the preschool. When her youngest left to go to school she applied for a paid position. Local authority funding enabled her to study for a Level 2 and then Level 3 qualification. Over time Anjum progressed to deputy leader and then manager of the setting. We might term Anjum an 'accidental practitioner'—she did not purposely seek out the career she finds herself in, although she finds she enjoys it since undertaking the role—and eventually finds herself in charge of a 48-place preschool.

Laura is 24 years old and graduated from university with a degree in early childhood studies. She quickly found employment at a large day nursery, first in a baby room and now as a room leader. She has been in this role for three years now although the hours are long and the pay is low. Laura feels there is little room for career progression in her current setting. She is beginning to make enquiries at teacher training providers locally about routes into teaching.

Simon is 30 years old and working in a Children's Centre. He has a foundation degree in early childhood education. Over his 12 years of work experience he has developed a finely tuned suite of skills that enable him to work effectively both with children and their families across a range of vulnerabilities. He is considering his next career move.

Debbie is a registered childminder. She is 54 years old with over 25 years of working with children of a variety of ages, in partnership with children's parents. She has no formal qualifications although she has regularly kept her professional development up to date by attending practice-oriented training sessions. The local authority had previously asked her to be a 'buddy childminder' for newly registering childminders; however, now they are only asking only those who have EYPS to undertake this role.

Reflection point 8.2

For each of the individuals above, how do you think they might have reacted to the introduction of EYPS (and then the move to EYTS) in relation to its signalling of the 'quality professional', and why?

You might like to consider:

- Might they see it as the opportunity to have their status recognised for aiding career progression, or 'another hoop they have to jump through?'

- Might they see it as an opportunity to develop their own practice even further, or question why they need to engage in further study in order to 'prove' (to whom?) what they already do?

- Might they see it as an opportunity for the early years sector to be seen as equitable to other stages in the education continuum, or might they see it as yet something more they have to do in order to strive to be equitable in the eyes of others in the field?

- Might they welcome the guidance of a set suite of standards to help them determine and ultimately validate their own professionalism, or might they refute the idea that there is a set 'recipe' to professional practice in the early years?

It could be argued that all of the above individuals are quality professionals, and yet each may or may not have a professional accreditation or qualification that states this. Colley (2006) and Taggart (2011) go so far as to suggest that far from increasing or recognizing professionalism, this approach actually seeks to 'exploit' those it is aimed at. This is because, as touched on earlier, the field is largely privatized—this means the government has led a situation whereby the majority of the early years provision is delivered within the private, voluntary and independent sector. Although some degree of 'control' has been retained, through Ofsted inspections for example, the fact remains that the actual delivery of provision has been relinquished by the government in all cases apart from a small percentage (*c.* 22 per cent) of maintained provisions. Furthermore, there are structural vulnerabilities at play—predominantly economical ones, because most settings rely heavily on government funding streams (2-, 3- and 4- year-old funding) for financial viability. Finally, there are social factors to consider, primarily the absence of a nationally enforced pay strategy, akin to that afforded to qualified teachers. Colley (2006) and Taggart (2011) highlight that instead, this lure of a 'professional status' along with its inference of a promise of equality (alongside other professions such as teaching) in reality does not deliver for reasons of the vulnerabilities touched on above.

Reflection point 8.3

To develop your own perspective on what constitutes 'professionalism' or 'professional practice' in early years, you are asked to return to your original notes from Chapter 1. Go back to the list you made early on in Chapter 1 about the key ingredients of quality provision. For each of them, complete the table below:

Quality ingredient identified	What behaviours demonstrate this within good quality early years practice?	What skills does a professional need in order to support or demonstrate this?	What are the personal attributes or characteristics of adults working in the early years that support or demonstrate this?
1			
2			
3			
. . .			

Consider the list you have created against the National Standards (Early Years): what are the similarities and differences, or is there anything missing? What might some of the reasons for differences and omissions be? To help with this, you may wish to consider what the UK government had in mind for early years, and its workforce, when they introduced EYPS and then EYTS at its inception.

Professionalism as more than a set of descriptors

Moyles (2001) provides us with an alternative idea of professionalism—the idea that professionalism is concerned with thinking about the facets of one's role and that in order to be 'professional', an individual should have high levels of professional knowledge, self-esteem and self-confidence. However, this suggests that to be 'professional' requires both role- and personal-related attributes—knowledge can, in the main, be taught and yet self-esteem and confidence tend to be something that one develops through experience. Professional knowledge, or the 'technical' understanding required to undertake a job role, is not inherent—individuals are not born with a predetermined knowledge suite; you are most likely reading this book in order to 'learn' some professional knowledge to help you in your practice. The development or acquisition of self-esteem and self-confidence are ambiguous both in terms of capturing their development and the nature of their development. Furthermore, 'softer' skills such as confidence, self-direction and empathy are tacit in nature, and as such are often not able to be reported, captured or measured either by oneself or others (Eraut 2000, 2004) so it is tricky to see how 'professionalism' could be defined by these when they are, by their nature, not easily measurable or definable. A specific knowledge set might be argued as being about informing professional practice, whereas self-esteem and confidence are more closely linked to professional identities. While one might be able to be explicitly defined, the latter proves more troublesome.

Reflection point 8.4

Look at the table above again. Which are accessed or delivered via technical ability and which are reliant on softer skills?

- Can all of these be learned or taught?
- How might the softer skills required be defined, measured, observed?
- Can all of your list be taught, or even defined in terms of how it could be measured? Which are intrinsic capabilities and which can be extrinsically taught?
- Are some negotiable, or must all of those aspects be in place to be a quality early years professional?

The notion of a generic 'professional identity', therefore, becomes problematic in terms of defining how it is constructed, and forms the topic of the following section where you will be invited to consider whether, in fact, the 'individual' can be separated from one's professional practice—whether it 'should' be separated—or are the two intertwined, inextricably linked or co-dependent in some way?

Professionals as 'experts'?

One perspective of a knowledge-centric response to what an early years professional is might lead to a response of either 'an expert' or someone within the field who demonstrates 'expertness' in their practice. Lave and Wenger's 'legitimate peripheral participation' paradigm was supported by Bereiter and Scardamalia (1993) whose earlier work had been centred around what defined an 'expert' and the stages that you go through in order to achieve 'expert status'. The possibility of a 'professional' being an 'expert' resonates with government suggestions that increased training and support for graduates in early years is the key vehicle for delivering a 'world-class early years sector' as discussed earlier. Bereiter and Scardamalia endorsed the practice of 'legitimate peripheral participation' based on their recognition of the importance of teamwork compared to individual learning. They defined 'experts' as 'those who can tackle problems that are beyond themselves' rather than fragmenting 'problems' into components, which are then addressed in isolation and handled with familiar routine (usually taught in a didactic fashion by another 'more able' person) by experts who construct new concepts and methods for dealing with unfamiliar and unexpected situations that arise. Considering the above vignette of Anjum, it might be argued her journey to her current role has been through a process of 'legitimate peripheral participation'—she started as a parent helper and worked alongside 'more expert others', developing her practice along the way through situated learning—learning within the real context of her field. She has now moved to a place of 'expertness' by taking on the manager role and leading the practice of others in the setting. Relating this to our above discussions about 'professional identities', Bereiter and Scardamalia's (1993) ideas, alongside what is offered to us from Lave and Wenger (1991), suggest that through developing this technical competence she would also, as a by-product, develop the personal competences required for the role—learning technical skills leads to the development of softer skills, too. In theory, this does not at first appear improbable; within the early years sector it is generally accepted that learning is a social learning process and so it would seem reasonable to consider that through immersion in the field, an individual might naturally 'pick up' or absorb the qualities and attributes generally held to be positive in that context.

While at a superficial level this suggests a somewhat ideological notion of learning, it is questionable whether it is applicable to the contemporary early years workplace, however, for reasons that we shall now explore. Eraut (2000, 2004) has written extensively about the 'obstacles' faced by many within the workplace—physical, psychological and social—particularly in relation to the acquisition of the tacit learning referred to above. Therefore, it is pertinent to deliberate on whether these obstacles might in fact become actual barriers to gaining the 'expertness' that Bereiter and Scardamalia (1993) speak of and to what Lave and Wenger (1991) offer as a somewhat ideological approach to learning in the workplace.

Reflection point 8.5

You are, therefore, now asked to reflect on what some of these obstacles to achieving that 'expert status' might be, considering government agendas of the past 10–15 years or so, before considering how this not only shapes ideologies of 'the professional' within early years but also more specifically about how this relates to the provision of 'quality practice'.

Lave and Wenger (1991) spoke about how professionals learn within their context; it was assumed this was a normative expectation that professionals within a job role would seek to continually improve; after all, why would they not seek a degree of expertness? Lave and Wenger purported that novices to the field start as onlookers of practice, observing the practice of others and gradually learning through an apprenticeship model—watching, observing and gradually doing. As individuals learn to 'do' more, they take an increased responsibility for their own practice, before ultimately being the 'more able' other who is then, in turn, observed by new novices to the field. Within leadership and management literature, however, Down had begun her writing with the explicit assumption that learning is largely a social activity, and although she agreed learning was a social process where everyone has a role to play in helping others, she also highlighted that: 'sometimes we are all unwittingly guilty of preventing another person from learning' (Down, 1995 p. 47).

The premise that 'everyone has a role to play in helping others to learn' provides a challenge to the previously held idea of 'experts' because it suggests that we are all experts in our own unique way. The principle that at times 'we are all unwittingly guilty of preventing another person from learning' reinforced the suggestions of Eraut's work about the different obstacles that individuals might face in the workplace, and begins to lead to a suggestion that other individuals—indeed, even 'experts' possibly—in that community might, in fact, be a preventative factor to professional development of others.

Reflection point 8.6

Consider your own route to being the 'professional' that you are today. Has every experience been positive, or have you faced some obstacles? Try to list the obstacles you have encountered. Have they been negative or positive? Have they helped or hindered your development?

The changing nature of the field of education, the recent government austerity measures and the professional, personal and political 'obstacles' at play means that Lave and Wenger's communities of practice paradigm now appears to offer a too simplistic view of the situation and context to be completely helpful for those developing a professional identity within early years services. Instead, the journey to being a professional in early years purports to be a much more complex and interwoven contemporary field from which to develop one's own practice and professionalism, and this—coupled with the political interference explored in the earliest part of this chapter—serves to make the job of defining just what or who an early years professional is trickier still.

In the middle of the 'professional' there is an 'I' . . .

To complicate this discussion even further, at the centre of every professional there is a human being, each with their own emotional dimension to their persona. As such, each professional has not only emotional responses to their professional experiences but also a degree of emotion that they bring to their role and to their field. Hoschschild (1983) wrote extensively about emotional aspect of 'beings', separating the notion of emotional work (the concept of managing one's own feelings and reformatting them into acceptable presentation for social situations) and emotional labour (where work and personal values sometimes conflict with one another). Mirchandani (2003) suggested that emotional work and emotional labour were so closely intertwined that they could not be separated. Given the nature of early years work, there is an appropriateness to discussing the emotional aspect of the field and the work undertaken—both directly with children but also of the effect on professionals themselves; we spoke earlier about a dichotomy between creativity and compliance, and it is likely that this will bring about a degree of emotionality. Martin (2005) provides us with the term 'emotional culture'. He spoke about the emotional culture of an organization (in this case, an early years setting) being a combination not only of the personal emotions that individuals feel but also extended this to consider the emotion of the setting or business as a whole. Martin suggested that it was as important to consider the emotions that professionals suppressed rather than displayed, and wrote about the emotional culture as being the 'unspoken rules', the 'norms' and the rituals that were present in a context and it was these attributes which created the emotional culture of a setting. We consider, therefore, once again that professionalism not only refers to technical knowledge or competence but also to personal or softer skills—and now to a dimension of 'unspoken' (perhaps even unknown to the individual?) cultural norms that help shape notions of 'professional' practices.

In parallel, Ashkanasy, Härtel, & Zerbe (2001, p. 93) write about sociological factors that affect the displaying of emotions in a work environment and refers to this in her writing about 'dominant norms'—the fact that (within the Western context) women are generally viewed as 'more' emotional as men that, in turn, allows a greater acceptance of women showing emotion in social situations. Despite various initiatives to increase the percentage of male worker in the field of early years, it remains a largely female-dominated workforce. It is generally considered, particularly in the workplace, that it is more permissible for women to show these types of emotion rather than men. This notion of what is more or less socially acceptable in terms of demonstrations of emotion is referred to as 'emotionology'—the production and reproduction of emotions that help us to learn, trough society and media, what is appropriate or inappropriate in relation to displays of emotion in social contexts (Colley, 2012). So, this adds to our ideas of what constructs a professional—technical capability, softer or tacit skills, and now also sociological norms of practice.

A drive to focus services to those in greatest needs and a general targeting of services for young children means thresholds for statutory services are generally rising. As a result, an increasing proportion of those children who might typically have been afforded the support of statutory safeguarding services no longer 'qualify'. However, their needs remain nonetheless. As the core 'universal' provision for early years children, the mantle, therefore, falls to early years professionals to support the needs of these children—and often their families, too. One cannot ignore (nor should they) the emotional aspect of undertaking work with such children who are vulnerable and in need of additional support. The sense of responsibility that those working in the field often feel further heightens this. Early years, therefore, can be an emotionally charged profession by its very nature. As a professional within the field, you will undoubtedly come into contact with young children and begin to learn and understand not only about them as individuals but often also about their family and home life, and for cases where additional vulnerabilities are at play that are at odds with what you would hope for the child, this can prove emotionally disruptive. With rising social care thresholds, contraction of other support services to children and their families, early years professionals are involved even more so than ever before with the child's life outside of the setting and to a greater degree than ever before. The role of an early years professional is, therefore, one that is malleable in nature—and not always intentionally so—but as a result of changes in other services.

The question of professional and personal persona, their interrelationships (or not) and whether one can be separated from one another is interesting when considering what it means to be a 'quality professional'.

In earlier chapters, and in this one, you have been invited to consider whether the 'quality' aspects are related to technical knowledge, understanding, skills or something entirely different. But, of course, all early years practitioners are individuals in their own right, and as such they experience emotions and are influenced by socially constructed norms of behaviour and practices. So, what sets quality professionals aside from everyone else in the field? To help you to understand this further, you need to think about the construct of the 'sense of self' in its most personal nature.

Francis (1999) recognizes 'the self' as a persuasive constituent of any professional role and goes on to explore the emotional aspect to working 'in the field'—in this case in the field of early years, and suggests to us that it is this emotion that not only continually constructs and reconstructs one's sense of self but also their construction of professional identity. In particular, Francis writes about the fine line between 'getting too close' and remaining marginal—an area explored in Chapter 2, 'Quality experiences for babies and very young children', where we considered the notion of 'professional love' in early years. While Coffey (1999) raises question with the appropriateness or necessity to consider one's sense of self before engaging in the field, Hammersley and Atkinson (1995, p. 115) warn against such surrender, instead maintaining that there should remain a degree of social and emotional distance between the individual and the field—as it is within this 'space' that the individual can analyse practice observed and experienced, and it is, therefore, here in this 'space' that understanding can be achieved. We begin to see an indication, therefore, as to how 'professionals' emerge from 'individuals' and begin to consider whether they are one and the same, or if, in fact, there should (or can be) distance between the two constructs.

Lofland and Lofland (1995) extend this discussion, and while we will not go into further depth here, it is worthy of consideration for further reading about the continual construction of self; emotionally, professionally and within professional relationships, because as an early years practitioner you will undoubtedly be engaging in professional relationships with a wide variety of 'stakeholders' in the child's life; parents, other professionals (health visitors, social workers, speech and language therapists, and so on) and, of course, others within your setting (including other childminders locally if you are a registered childminder).

The concept of what an early years professional 'is', therefore, becomes all the more important for several reasons. Jack and Donnellan (2010) alerted leaders of practice that a failure to recognize the 'person within' was deemed to have a detrimental effect on the individuals' well-being, and with this brings about increased staff stress, morale and, therefore, turnover. Emotion in the workplace is, therefore, a highly complex subject, and one that has only been touched on here, but it is important to recognize and consider in this respect how quality professionals are constructed and also in how they develop their own resilience to such effects and how they contribute to ensuring the resilience of others around them in the setting. Professionalism, therefore, becomes a matter of not only enabling and empowering others to develop technical and tacit capabilities but also of ensuring one's own resilience.

It might be argued that at the most fundamental level, therefore, that an early years professional is someone who:

- recognizes both their areas of 'expertness' but also areas in which they are less 'expert in'—and seeks to continually improve in all
- recognizes the influences at play within their field, including the emotional impact of such influences
- seeks to continue to deliver practice that is congruent with their knowledge and understanding of what is right and appropriate for young children
- seeks to continually develop their own skill set—professionally and personally —both of themselves and others
- and does so in such a way that the viability of the setting is not compromised

In short, therefore, if we are considering what a 'quality professional' in early years is, it is surely someone that recognizes these political dimensions and their influences, understands how this can influence practice (both positively and negatively) and seeks to mitigate and negotiate such influences into practice that upholds what is understood to be appropriate and effective for young children's learning and development, both in the immediate and longer term. Not only does this apply to their relationships with themselves, others around them (adults and children) but in the wider professional field.

Multi-agency working

Despite the malleable nature that those working in the field of early years find themselves, there is a widely accepted paradigm that multi-agency working is the 'better' and 'more effective' way of working, and this is supported by findings of numerous research reports (CAIPE, 1997; Department for Education and

Skills, 2004, 2005, 2006b, 2007; National Evaluation of Sure Start, 2008; Simmons, Siraj-Blatchford, Melhuish, & Taggart, 2008). We use the term 'multi-agency' here but you might also see phrases such as inter-agency, interdisciplinary, multidisciplinary and multi-professional used. While there are discreet nuances between such terms, we generally consider here that the terms refer to working in partnership with another agency outside of the immediate setting (health visitors, social workers, speech and language therapists, family support workers, local voluntary services, and so on). To consider what this looks like in practice, we consider that multi-agency working is generally embodied by the notion of children (and their families) having access to a wider range of services and support mechanism that are immediately available from within your acute context (Gasper, 2011). The benefit of such practice is that they are supported to:

- identify what their needs are
- access the most appropriate help from relevant agencies
- begin to take greater control of their own lives
- increase their confidence and self-worth
- develop their skills and education
- enable them to live fulfilled lives and contribute more fully to wider society. (Gasper, 2011, p. 2)

As an experienced practitioner, you may be reading this thinking, 'but this has always been the case—this isn't anything new'. While this may well be the case, the political emphasis to increase inter-agency collaboration was demonstrated by two successive key articles that initially focused on the safeguarding of children 'at risk' but which had ramifications for the children's services sector as a whole. These two articles were: 'Working together: A guide to arrangements for inter-agency co-operation for the protection of children from abuse' (Department of Health and Social Security, 1986) and 'Working together to safeguard children: A guide to inter-agency working to safeguard and promote the welfare of children' (Department of Health, the Home Office and Department for Education and Employment, 2006). Two notable areas of interest from the latter publication are first, multi-authored and jointly published by the three key government agencies of their time that worked with children and their families, and second, as the title suggests, a move away from simply seeing a need for inter-agency working where immediate and significant risks are present, but instead the expectation that this will happen to 'promote welfare' of children more widely. Achieving a high degree of evaluation and scrutiny, several reports celebrated the benefits that this way of working achieved (Anning, Stuart, Nicholls, Goldthorpe, & Morley, 2007). While the 'practice benefits' were substantial there is, of course, also a financial benefit to such practice. A recognition of the fact that working in a multi-agency way not only reduces duplication (both of the professionals involved but also for the family), this also, in turn, is likely to bring about financial costs savings—the higher up the 'tier of need' services are the more costly they generally become—both in monetary value and also in emotional cost to the family and ultimately the child.

Broffenbrenner (1996) provides an explanation of how this approach to working interacts with children's 'real-life' experiences through 'ecological systems' and 'proximal processes'—the interaction, by the child, with people, places, contexts and situations. Gasper (2011) suggests, therefore, that given this, quality professionals would need to 'embody attributes and attitudes that are principled and sensitive . . . considerate and reflective, better grounded in development of knowledge' (p. 112), thus contributing towards contexts, and that are creative, evaluative and adaptable as a result. Even more importantly, they need to be willing to redesign, perhaps continually, in response to changing needs of the sector and, of course, of children (2011, p. 112). One should not underestimate the complexity of this. While we need not be reminded of the consequence of not working in this way; the Lord Laming Report on the death of Victoria Climbie (Laming, 2003) made very clear that the lack of a 'joined-up' approach to safeguarding Victoria's death was a contributory factor to her death, this is not to say it is without challenge. The more recent 'Baby P case' (2007) shows that despite legislative frameworks that demand agencies should work together, it does not always 'get it right', nor is it a foolproof method of ensuring all children's safety and well-being. A multi-agency approach is almost impossible if all agencies are not involved wholeheartedly. However, given that we have spent the majority of this chapter uncovering the array of factors that have an influence on a constructed image of an 'early years professional', if we then consider this uncertainty times the number of professionals aiming to work in this complex multi-agency manner, then an even more complex web of practice illuminates. Furthermore, as we have already identified that each individual will need to continually construct and then reconstruct their professional identity through their responses to a range of experiences and influences, it becomes all the more likely that one single construct of an 'early years professional' may ever be defined. The importance, therefore, lies in you as an individual recognizing the 'mess' and complexity of the field you are working in, or seeking to work in, and creating your own professional identity that ensures the best possible outcome for children in your care, despite the complex mess that is surrounding—and trying to influence—your daily practice with those children and in the sector as a whole.

References

Ahlbäck Öberg, S., & Bringselius, L. (2014). Professionalism and organizational performance in the wake of new managerialism. *European Political Science Review*, 1–25.

Allen, G. (2011). *Early intervention: The next steps*: *An independent report to Her Majesty's Government*. London: Her Majesty's Government.

Anning, A., Stuart, J., Nicholls, M., Goldthorpe, J., & Morely, A. (2007). *Understanding variations in effectiveness among Sure Start Local Programmes: Final Report*. London: Department for Education and Skills (DfES).

Arnaboldi, M., & Lapsley, I. (2008). Making management available: The implementation of best value in local government. *Abacus, 44*(1), 1–27.

Arnaboldi, M., Lapsley, I., & Steccolini, I. (2015). Performance management in the public sector: The ultimate challenge. *Financial Accountability & Management, 31*(1), 1–22.

Ashkanasy, N. M., Härtel, C. E. J., & Zerbe, W. J. (2001). *Emotions in the workplace: Research, theory and practice*. Westport, CT: Qurum Books.

Banks, S. (2013). Ethics in an age of austerity: Social work and the evolving new public management. *Journal of Social Intervention: Theory and Practice, 20*(2), 5–23.

Bereiter, C., & Scardamalia, M. (1993). *Surpassing ourselves: An inquiry into the notion of expertise*. La Salle, IL: Open Court.

Broffenbrenner, U. (1996). *The ecology of human development*. London: Harvard University Press.

CAIPE (1997) Interprofessional education: A definition. London: Centre for the Advancement of Inter-professional Education (p. 9). In H. Barr, I. Koppel, S. Reeves, M. Hammicj, & D. Freeth (2005) *Effective inter-professional education: Argument, assumption and evidence* (p. 17). Oxford: Blackwell/CAIPE.

Coffey, A. (1999). *The ethnographic self: Fieldwork and the representation of identity*. London: Sage.

Colley, H. (2006). Learning to labour with feelings: Class, gender and emotions in childcare, education and training. *Contemporary Issues in Early Childhood, 7*(1), 15–29.

Colley, H. (2012). Not learning in the workplace: Austerity and the shattering of illusion in public service work. *Journal of Workplace Learning, 24*(5), 317–333.

Department for Education. (2012). *Foundations for quality: The review of early education and childcare qualifications: Final Report*. Retrieved January 2, 2016, from https://www.education.gov.uk/publications/standard/Early Yearseducationandchildcare/Page1/DFE-00068-2-12

Department for Education. (2013). *More great childcare: Raising quality and giving parents more choice*. Retrieved on January 3, 2016, from https://www.education.gov.uk/publications/standard/publicationDetail/Page1/DFE-00002-2013

Department for Education. (2014). *The statutory framework for the early years foundation stage*. London: DfE.

Department for Education and Employment. (2008). *The statutory framework for the early years foundation stage*. London: DfEE.

Department for Education and Science. (2005). *Early impacts of Sure Start for children and families*. Research report NESS/2005/FR/013. London: Her Majesty's Stationery Office (HMSO).

Department for Education and Skills. (2004). *Every child matters: Change for children*. Nottingham: DfES Publications.

Department for Education and Skills (DfES). (2006a). *Children's workforce strategy: A strategy to build a world-class workforce for children and young people*. Nottingham: DfES Publications.

Department for Education and Skills (DfES). (2006b). *The early years foundation stage: Consultation on a single quality framework for services for children birth to three*. Nottingham: DfES Publications.

Department for Education and Skills. (2007). *Understanding variations in effectiveness amongst Sure Start Local Programmes: Final Report*, NESS/2007/SF/024. London: DfES.

Department of Health and Social Security. (1986).*Working together: A guide to arrangements for inter-agency co-operation for the protection of children from abuse*. London: Her Majesty's Government.

Department of Health, Home Office and Department for Education and Employment. (2006). *Working together to safeguard children: A guide to inter-agency working to safeguard and promote the welfare of children*. London: Her Majesty's Government.

Downs, S. (1995). *Learning at work: Effective strategies for making things happen*. London: Kogan Page.

Eraut, M. (2000). Non-formal learning and tacit knowledge in professional work. *British Journal of Educational Psychology, 70*(1), 113–136.

Eraut, M. (2004). Informal learning in the workplace. *Studies in Continuing Education, 26*(2), 247–273.

Eraut, M. (2004). Transfer of knowledge between education and workplace settings. In H. Rainbird, A. Fuller, & A. Munro (Eds.), *Workplace learning in context* (pp. 201–221). London and New York: Routledge.

Francis, B. (1999). Modernist reductionism or post-structuralist relativism—can we move on? An evaluation of the arguments in relation to feminist education research. *Gender and Education, 11*(4), 381–393.

Gasper, M. (2011). *Multi-agency working in the early years*. London: Sage.

Hammersley, M., & Atkinson, P. (1995). *Ethnography: Principles in practice* (2nd ed.). London: Routledge.

Hoschschild, A. R. (1983). *The managed heart: Commersialisation of human feelings*. Berkley, CA: University of California Press.

Jack, G., & Donnellan, H. (2010). Recognising the person within the developing professional: Tracking the early careers of newly qualified child care social workers in three local authorities in England. *Social Work Education, 29*(3), 305–318.

Laming, H. (2003). *The Victoria Climbie inquiry.* London: Her Majesty's Stationery Office (HMSO).

Lave, J., & Wenger, E. (1991). *Situated learning: Legitimate peripheral participation* Cambridge: Cambridge University Press.

Lofland, J., & Lowland, L. H. (1995). *Analysing social settings: A guide to qualitative observation and analysis.* Belmont, CA: Wadsworth Publishing, Inc.

Lynch, K., Grummell, B., & Lyons, M. (2012). *New managerialism in education: Commercialization, carelessness, and gender.* Basingstoke: Palgrave Macmillan.

Martin, A. (2005). The role of positive psychology in enhancing satisfaction, motivations and productivity in the workplace. *Journal of Organisational Behaviour Management, 24*(1), 113–131.

Mirchandani, K. (2003). *Making Americans: Transnational call centre work in India.* Toronto, Canada: University of Toronto.

Moyles, J. (2001). Passion, paradox and professionalism in early years education. *Early Years, 21*(2), 81–95.

National Evaluation of Sure Start Research Team (2008) *The impact of Sure Start Local Programmes on three-year-olds and their families: Research Report.* Retrieved on October 19, 2015, from NESS/2008/FR/027 website: www.ness. bbk.ac.uk/documents/activities/impact/41.pdf

Oberheumer, P. (2005). Conceptualising the early childhood pedagogue: Policy approaches and issues of professionalism. *European Early Childhood Education Research Journal, 13*(1), 5–16.

Oberheumer, P., & Shreyer, P., & Neuman, M. J. (2010). *Professionals in early childhood education and care systems: European profiles and perspectives.* Opaden, Germany: Barbara Budricj Publishers.

Osgood, J. (2011). Deconstructing professionalism in early childhood education: Resisting the regulatory gaze. *Contemporary Issues in Early Childhood, 7*(1), 5–14.

Pugh, G. (2010). The policy agenda for early childhood services. In G. Pugh & B. Duffy (Eds.), *Contemporary issues in the early years* (6th ed.). London: Sage.

Simmons, P., Siraj-Blatchford, I., Melhuish, E., & Taggart, B. (2008). Is public investment in the early years worthwhile? *Early Education, 54*(1), 3–4.

Taggart, G. (2011). Don't we care?: The ethics and emotional labour of early years professionalism. *Early Years, 31*(1), 85–95.

9 International perspectives on quality in early years education

Patrick Carmichael

In this book we have been primarily concerned with early years education and care in a UK context—and specifically in relation to frameworks and guidance that apply in early years settings in England, as there are distinctive and different aspects to provision in other parts of the UK. In other chapters we have alluded to practice in other countries, but in this chapter we will consider more systematically some international perspectives that have had a significant impact on early years practice and notions of quality, as well as locating UK practice in a broader, global context. We will do this by thinking both about *quality as measured*, exploring the way in which international comparisons have shaped our notions of quality practice and children's entitlements to early years education and care; and *quality as exemplified*, considering influential traditions and innovative practice from around the world.

The visions of early years education and care that are expressed in the Early Years Foundation Stage and the various frameworks for measuring and improving quality practice and provision themselves draw on a range of ideas, theories and traditions about early childhood (not just early years education) from different periods in history and from around the world. And with these come views of what high-quality early years provision might mean; in some cases, with sharing and 'borrowing' of ideas, concepts and practice across these theories and traditions; in other cases, offering distinctively different perspectives that do not seem to be reconcilable and present professionals with dilemmas and challenges.

When we look at early years settings, we often take for granted many of the activities we see and the resources that accompany them. The presence of unit blocks and other sets of objects for building and reconfiguration owes much to the pioneering work of Froebel who, in turn, drew on the earlier work of Pestalozzi, and introduced his *spielgabe* ('play gifts') to kindergartens at a time—the first half of the nineteenth century—when early learning was largely conceived as involving books and instruction, rather than as having play and games at its core (Brosterman, 1997). Free-flow early years environments and the view that even very young children can choose activities and decide for how long they continue with them reflects the lasting influence of Maria Montessori on thinking about the design and social organization of learning environments, and the division of learning environments into spaces with distinctive educational, rather than simply organizational, intentions is also characteristic of Montessori's ideas. More recent initiatives such as 'Forest Schools' (Blackwell & Pound, 2011) also draw on a rich international heritage, with their advocates citing the influence of nineteenth-century American educators such as Emerson and Thoreau, alongside the 'open-air' movement of Margaret Macmillan and more contemporary advocates of critical 'eco-pedagogy' such as Richard Kahn (2010). And broader ideas of participatory democracy in education, even where young children are involved, and the view that education needs to be underpinned by commitments to care, love and respect (as discussed in several of the previous chapters in this book) are strongly influenced by the work of the Brazilian educator, Paolo Freire (Watling & Clarke, 1995). Early years settings, together with the practice of early years professionals and the notions of quality that accompany them, cannot be seen in isolation from this rich, varied, and sometimes contested and contradictory, international heritage.

These traditions, as well as having their own variations and contradictions, also may be at odds with curricula, standards and notions of quality that are driven by other political, social and economic agendas. While some early years curricula may be couched in terms of 'preparation' for subsequent schooling, or may use the idea of a 'spiral curriculum' in which early learning introduces skills and dispositions that will be revisited in later schooling, the motivations of many of the thinkers mentioned was to establish early years education as something continuous with other life experience. Freire, for example, was clear that education was one of a number of forms of social inclusion and a means by which the experience of democratic participation could be introduced, even from an early age.

Reflection point 9.1

Reflect on your own practice and that which you have observed in your setting or settings. Where can you see the evidence of these diverse traditions of early years education? Is the 'heritage' of practices, resources and language, and the rationale behind them made explicit; or are these things that we just 'do' in early years?

Quality as measured and quality as exemplified

It is beyond the scope of this book to offer a review of global patterns in early years education and care, or even a review of all of the ways in which quality is conceptualized or measured around the world. So what the remainder of this chapter will offer are two ways in which we can look beyond our local settings and learn, as professionals, from international perspectives—in addition to all of the historical movements and currents of thought indicated above that have found their way into early years practice.

The first way is to draw on international frameworks that define the fundamental rights of children, even very young children, and which, in turn, allow international comparisons of actual provision and practice. Often, these are framed by the same international frameworks, and provide us with examples of how fundamental rights can be addressed and even exceeded, but, sadly, in others they document failures to provide even the most basic standards of care and education for babies, children and their families. This approach allows us to think about *quality as measured* and allows us to compare provision with that elsewhere in the world in terms of key indicators.

The second way in which we can draw on international perspectives is to learn about instances of thoughtful (and often inspirational) early years provision that engages creatively (and sometimes in very radical ways) with notions of childhood, learning, care, and what it means to be an early years professional or teacher. This is *quality as exemplified*.

Quality as measured

An important foundation for thinking about the standards of care and education to which all children, including the youngest, should be entitled is the United Nations Convention on the Rights of the Child (United Nations Children's Fund, 2014; United Nations General Assembly, 1989). This sets out four basic principles:

- the right not to be discriminated against
- the right to life, survival and development
- devotion to the best interests of the child
- respect for the views of the child

Access to education is, therefore, seen as part of a broader set of rights and entitlements, and this has driven global initiatives such as those to provide universal primary education and to address inequities in the enrolment in school of girls, ethnic and religious minorities and children with disabilities (United Nations Children's Fund, 2000). This has not proved easy, however, as global and regional initiatives have often proved difficult to reconcile with local cultural practices and disruption to civil society (including educational systems) due to poverty, war and environmental factors. One very significant development, driven in part by the difficulties in offering universal access to education and care, is a more recent move towards thinking not simply about the 'entitlement' to education (which does not, of course, ensure its quality) but rather 'school readiness' which according to the United Nations definition involves:

> Children's readiness for school; school's readiness for children; and families' readiness for school. Together, these pillars bolster children's likelihood of success. Children's readiness for school affects their learning and development. Schools' readiness for children ensures learning environments are child-friendly and adapt to the diverse needs of

young learners and their families. In turn, families' readiness for school connotes a positive and supportive approach to education, their children's learning and the transition from home to school. (United Nations Children's Fund, 2011)

This broader definition of the relationship between school, family and child, and 'child-friendly schooling' (United Nations Children's Fund, 2010) means that as well as supporting more formal early years settings and linking them to the later school system:

In countries with a tradition of community childcare, UNICEF promotes community-based early childhood care and development programmes . . . this approach may also entail training traditional caregivers in up-to-date practices. (United Nations Children's Fund, 2011)

It is important to recognize here that there is no simple 'divide' between more economically developed countries (such as those in Europe and North America) and 'traditional' approaches in less economically developed areas. How early years education and care is conceptualized varies widely and it is notable that some of the most economically advanced and socially equitable economies have approaches to early years provision and practice that privilege community learning and support over formal learning. We will look at some examples of this later in this chapter. What this means, though, is that simple indicators, such as percentage enrolments, years spent in formal schooling, or any comparisons of children's skills and achievements, may mask complex social and cultural patterns, so it is important not to make assumptions based on the current pattern of provision in western Europe, the UK, or even just in England. Better indicators might then be the numbers of professionals engaged in early years care, support and education regardless of whether this happens in formal or 'community' settings; the proportion of government spending that goes to early years provision; or the investments made in training new early years professionals.

Reflection point 9.2

Many educational settings display excerpts from the United Nations Convention on the Rights of the Child, or explicitly incorporate these into policy documents.

* How are these related to school policy and enacted in practice?
* How are they conveyed to parents and carers, to new staff, and to children?
* How can something as conceptually complex as 'rights' be conveyed to young children?

In order to determine those areas where these universal rights are not recognized, guaranteed or are under threat, and to inform global development priorities, international data are collected by agencies such as the United Nations Economic, Scientific and Cultural Organization (UNESCO), the World Bank and the Organization for Economic Co-operation and Development (OECD), both in the form of large-scale quantitative data sets and case studies of regions, countries and initiatives. The challenge, of course, just as with 'quality', is how to quantify 'rights', and a range of measurable 'proxy variables' are used alongside direct measurements and qualitative accounts.

One of the most comprehensive studies that attempts to draw together all these kinds of data and quality indicators was a report entitled *Starting Well*, published by the Economist Intelligence Unit (2012). This uses a range of indicators, some of which are concerned with legal rights (such as the right to access preschool education, in accordance with the United Nations Convention) while others measure provision, investment and enrolment, in order to provide rankings of early years provision. The Economist Intelligence Unit report draws attention to the correlations between early years provision and quality, and other political, social and economic indicators and further states that:

> Few countries today prioritise education spending towards the preschool stage. Budgets typically follow an inverted pyramid model, with most funding going to secondary and tertiary levels, with the least to preschool. (2012, p. 18)

The report draws attention to well-established and effective systems that 'rank' highly, highlighting patterns of provision in the Nordic countries in particular:

> Finland, Sweden and Norway top the Index, thanks to sustained, long-term investments and prioritisation of early childhood development, which is now deeply embedded in society. (Economist Intelligence Unit, 2012, p. 6)

The report also highlights countries, such as Chile and the Czech Republic, which perform well against the ranking criteria despite financial strictures and cites examples of early years initiatives in Vietnam and Greece (Economist Intelligence Unit, 2012, p. 6).

Another interesting perspective on global indicators is provided by the *Gapminder* project that takes comparative international data sets including those from the United Nations, the World Bank, the OECD and other agencies and allows their comparison using an elegant online interface (Gapminder, 2015). It is possible to explore how educational measures correlate with other social, economic and political indicators both now and over time; what emerges are clear pictures of how limited or unequal early years provision and outcomes are, in many cases, closely related to broader patterns of income, health, security and gender equity:

lack of access to early years care and provision is a key part of the global epide-
miology of poverty and inequity. At the same time, it is interesting to see how, in
some parts of the world, major initiatives have reduced levels of infant mortality,
improved public knowledge about young children's needs and enabled access to
education. The 'outliers' that do not conform to general patterns are worthy of
further investigation as they may provide *exemplifications* of how early years
provision and practice elsewhere in the world might influence our own notions of
quality and offer solutions to some of the challenges we face. We will now turn our
attention to some of these examples.

Reflection point 9.3

What are the 'key indicators' that you are concerned with in your settings?
Are they 'inputs' (such as measures of social deprivation, receipt of pupil
premium, parental occupation) or 'outputs' (such as attendance or achievement)? How complete a picture of the quality of the provision can these
provide without further contextual information?

Quality as exemplified

We will look at four examples of systems with different patterns of early years
provision and differing theoretical and conceptual frameworks for understanding
the experience of children and the notion of quality. These are the well-known
preschool and primary school system of the municipality of Reggio Emilia in
northern Italy, which has had a far-reaching influence on early years provision
elsewhere; the early Childhood Education and Care (ECEC) system of Sweden
(highlighted in the *Starting well* report); the community- and child-centred *Te
Whrāiki* curriculum of New Zealand; and, representing an unusual case of an
economically constrained but effective participatory model, the Early Childhood
Care and Education (ECCE) programmes of Cuba.

The preschools of the municipality of Reggio Emilia

We have already discussed the educational system of the municipality of Reggio
Emilia in Chapter 3 on quality environments, but there is much more to the
approaches used in the schools of the Reggio Emilia and those elsewhere in the
world that have drawn on their philosophy and practice.

Established after the Second World War, the Reggio Emilia approach is strongly
'rights-based' and stems from a belief that all children have the right not only to
receive preschool education, but also that they have the right to a say in what
and how they learn, and to develop their potential through self-directed and carefully guided social interactions with adults and other children (Malaguzzi, 1993):

the term 'a pedagogy of relationships' features widely in writing by practitioners of the approach. 'Influenced by this belief', writes Hewitt (2001, p. 96), 'the child is beheld as beautiful, powerful, competent, creative, curious, and full of potential and ambitious desires.' Following on from this, emphasis is placed on the intensity and quality of each child's learning:

> We can concentrate on quality rather than quantity. Children need not experience a large number of different educational experiences in one day but rather should be given the time and space to develop learning in depth. The [Reggio Emilia] Curriculum Framework is helpful in this aspect, stating that planning should be flexible so that it can take account of children's ideas and responses to learning experiences and allow learning to develop spontaneously. (Learning and Teaching Scotland, 2006, p. 31)

Much has been written about the Reggio Emilia approach, but it is interesting that what is identified by actual practitioners as contributing to its success and to the quality of the children's experience is this firm grounding in a commitment to children's rights; and to practitioner reflection, both as an intrinsic aspect of everyday practice and longer-term staff development. Carlina Rinaldi explains that:

> Good staff development is not something that is undertaken every now and then, reflecting only on the words of someone else. Instead, it is a vital and daily aspect of our work, of our personal and professional identities. Staff development is seen above all as an indispensable vehicle by which to make stronger the quality of our interaction with children and among ourselves. (Learning and Teaching Scotland, 2006, p. 20)

Initial teacher education, particularly in relation to early years, was poorly developed until the 1990s in Italy, and when the University of Modena established a Faculty of Education to address this, they involved Reggio Emilia practitioners, including Rinaldi, to develop their training programmes. This is an atypical arrangement by which professional practice, established over decades and recognized as being of high quality by both academic commentators and the community it serves, informs or influences teacher training. And, as such, it is rather different from the model of government mandating standards and higher education institutions being inspected as to how well they prepare new professionals to address them!

Early Childhood Education and Care in Sweden

There are similarities between the Reggio Emilia approach and the ways in which the Nordic (Scandinavian) countries have developed their early years practice. There is a strong sense of 'entitlement' and partnership between the state, teachers and parents. The OECD has produced a series of reports and country case studies; in part because of the continued success of these countries in international comparisons such as the *Starting Well* survey described earlier. The OECD reports highlight the fact that:

> The Nordic approach is very different to seeing [Early Childhood Education and Care] as primarily an investment in the future, strongly linked to utilitarian ends, e.g. preparation for school (and later work), in which the child is considered as a person to be formed, rather than as a citizen who actively participates in the life of the ECEC centre. (Organization for Economic Co-operation and Development, 2001)

There is, once again, a highly rights-based underpinning here: to even talk about the young child as a participating 'citizen' makes this clear, and from this it follows that any notion of quality will be based on the extent to which these rights are recognized and acted on, the nature of the participation that is enabled and encouraged, and the contribution that ECEC makes to the life of the child, their family and their community.

The OECD country case study of Sweden (Taguma, Litjens, & Makowiecki, 2013) provides a detailed account of how this is implemented in practice. This document highlights how a national, legally binding curriculum has been put in place that:

- [puts] the child and play at the centre of the curriculum
- [balances] content by addressing academic and socio-emotional development
- [reflects] parental opinions and expectations
- [addresses] respect for cultural values. (Taguma et al., 2013, p. 8)

Broader social democratic principles extend beyond children's experience then; the third and fourth points listed above highlight that:

> partnership and parental engagement are important aspects of ECEC curricula: parents can be an important source of constructive feedback and input to ECEC programmes. Co-operation between preschools and parents ensures that children receive the opportunity of developing in accordance with children's potential. Parents' feedback, consultation and interaction with a service provider and ECEC staff can contribute to making parental preferences an important input of ECEC frameworks, and their opinions and expectations can be reflected in the curriculum. (Taguma et al., 2013, p. 32)

In the Swedish context, this means that early years professionals are expected to be sensitive to the cultural views and norms of different groups, including those in which ECEC has traditionally been within the family or community rather than within distinct early years settings. Historically, this has meant the Sami people of northern Sweden; but it could be argued that having a statutory early years framework that sees this respect for diverse cultural values and parental opinions as intrinsic aspects of quality already in place has prepared Sweden for the increasing numbers of migrants settling in Sweden as a result of mobility within the European Union (EU) as well as those fleeing war and persecution in the Middle East.

It is important to recognize, though, that the Nordic countries, including Sweden, are not solely concerned with providing a play-centred environment for young children, within a socially equitable and culturally sensitive context. There is also a concern of how best to bridge the gap from early years settings into primary schooling in Sweden with: 'a special preparatory year, or pre-school class, for 6- to 7- year-old children in the year before they enter compulsory school. This class prolongs the learning approaches of the kindergarten into the first years of the primary school' (Organization for Economic Co-operation and Development, 2006, p. 69). This has an interesting 'quality' dimension: it represents a recognition not only that transition between educational settings and phases is important, and that there is an element of 'preparation' in what goes on, but also that there are elements of early years practice that have something to contribute to discussions about the curriculum, learning and child development in later phases of the educational system.

Te Whāriki in New Zealand

Unlike the Swedish curriculum, the *Te Whāriki* curriculum introduced in the mid-1990s (New Zealand Ministry of Education, 1996) is not legally binding, and so allows more flexibility in content and delivery. At its core is an emphasis on the importance of belonging to a community and society:

> The Te Whāriki curriculum of New Zealand emphasises the critical role of socially and culturally mediated learning and of reciprocal and responsive relationships for children with people, places and things. Te Whāriki is founded on the aspirations for all children in New Zealand to grow up as competent and confident learners and communicators, healthy in mind, body and spirit, secure in their sense of belonging and in the knowledge that they make a valued contribution to society, indicating that the upbringing of children is a community-wide responsibility. (Organization for Economic Co-operation and Development, 2006, p. 69)

Te Whāriki includes a Māori immersion curriculum to recognize and meet the needs of the Māori population, and it also addresses the Tagata Pasifika culture to ensure that the language and culture of the Māori and Pasifika is protected, respected and supported. The curriculum is, therefore, bilingual and multicultural, developed in both the English and Māori languages, and is underpinned by a view that even very young children make a contribution to the educational settings, the community and the broader society in which they are cared for and in which they learn.

An important aspect of Te Whāriki in relation to quality and the evaluation is that the success of any initiative within it is the use of a common framework for both planning and evaluation. This constructive alignment (whereby activities, goals and outcomes 'align' and both adults and children can engage in reflective and evaluative dialogue) is focused around 'five questions', each relating to a key aspect of quality practice:

- Do you know me? (Belonging)
- Can I trust you? (Well-being)
- Do you let me fly? (Exploration)
- Do you hear me? (Communication)
- Is this place fair for us? (Contribution) (Podmore, May, & Carr, 2001)

The value of these apparently simple but actually very profound questions is that they can be used as a framing for enquiry at all levels from wide-ranging programme evaluation, in which case the questions might be asked by about a whole community, to reflection at the level of a setting, team or even an individual child.

Community education in Cuba

Our final example, that of Cuba, shares many features in common with the three examples we have already discussed: a commitment to a child-centred approach, a view of early years education as being 'in and of' the community rather than apart from it, and a belief that early years education has intrinsic social value aside from any preparation for school and work. What sets Cuba apart is its unusual economic and political situation; still guided by Marxist principles, its education system has had to develop in isolation from many of the sources of support available to other countries and education systems. This combination of factors has led to distinctive practice in education as in many other fields, where engagement in social action programmes and self-sufficiency are the norm.

The early years system in Cuba, then, includes several areas of interest, which we will briefly explore here. While education is compulsory in Cuba from the age of 6, early years care is available from birth and almost all children are enrolled in education from the age of 3 (United Nations Economic, Scientific and Cultural Organization, 2006, pp. 2–3). This significantly exceeds most other countries in the region and with a similar economic profile. In urban areas, provision generally takes the form of 'Children's Circles', the first of which was established in 1961, and the leaders of which are graduate early years specialists trained at the Latin American and Caribbean Pedagogical Institute in Havana (Tinajero,

2010, p. 6). The curriculum incorporates play but is not 'play-based' as such, but the strong links to the local community means that much activity takes place outside the formal setting, drawing on local resources and support from community organizations.

For those children who do not attend 'Children's Circles', early years education takes place in less formal early learning centres co-ordinated by the Local Network of Child Development Services. In terms of its aims and the range of services it offers, these have some similarities with Children's Centres in England, but they are for the most part run by local communities as part of social mobilization programmes, one of which is known as 'Educate Your Child'. Tinajero (2010, p. 10) writes that:

> The community, people's organizations, and agencies of the Central Administration of the State participate through the assemblies of people's power, local councils, local health councils, and coordinating groups for the different national programs. Coordinating groups for 'Educate Your Child' composed of representatives from various sectors exist at the national, provincial, municipal, and local levels.

To understand the 'Educate Your Child' programme, it is important to appreciate that this is not some kind of home-schooling initiative, nor a mechanism by which parents and carers are expected to prepare their children for entry into more formal early years settings, or compulsory schooling at 6 years old. Rather, it reflects a view of education, health and social care as a collective responsibility and something in which all members of a community are expected to take part. As such, early years professionals and local facilitators work with parents and carers so that they can contribute not only to their own child's care and learning, but those of the local community as well, and as such they are described as 'co-educators'. Support for parents to become community-based 'co-educators' is provided through the centres themselves, through training offered through the Pedagogical Institute and through the mass media (TV, radio, newspapers and magazines). The latter are particularly important in reaching parents in rural areas.

How then is 'quality' assessed in such a programme? While there are broad frameworks in place to ensure minimum standards, ensuring quality too is both a community responsibility and an aspect of social action. The quality of each area's 'Educate Your Child' programme is assessed by a co-ordinating group, which not only evaluates but also plans and mobilizes:

> The members of the coordinating groups are not necessarily educators, but group coordinators usually are. Coordinating groups at all levels generally meet once a month to discuss issues related to program operations. They answer to the Ministry of Education regarding regulatory and methodological matters and to the corresponding assembly of

people's power (national, provincial, or municipal level) regarding operational and administrative matters. The local coordinating groups call on people's organizations, communities, and families to analyze the progress of local plans. The promoters provide pedagogical guidance to the local groups and may request specific resources from them to ensure the quality of the educational process (for example, artists to take part in a community festival, new facilitators, cultural community events, and so forth). (Tinajero, 2010, p. 13)

This model goes beyond the notions of partnership and community involvement with which we may be familiar; early years education in Cuba is intensely 'political' with parents and carers fully involved alongside educational professionals who are both supported by, but answerable to, their local communities as much as central government.

The Cuban approach is not offered here as being ideal—it is not. Much of the practice is based as much on pragmatic decisions about what is possible with limited resources as it is on political ideology, and in some respects early years provision in Cuba has suffered from its political and economic isolation. But it does offer an interesting and sometimes inspiring counterpoint to centralized and mandated models of provision (often very well funded) within which key stakeholders (professionals, parents and carers, and children themselves) have little voice in shaping policy or establishing what is meant by quality.

Reflection point 9.4

At the opening of this chapter, we discussed how early years practice has absorbed ideas from diverse traditions and cultural settings. In our exemplifications we have highlighted (from a wide range of practice) some more approaches:

- From Italy: the idea of established professionals having an input into the training programmes of new early years teachers.

- From Sweden: the idea that early years is not just a preparation for formal schooling, but offers insights and approaches with wider and longer-term relevance, and so active transition strategies are needed.

- From New Zealand: an explicit recognition of the diverse cultural capital that even the youngest children bring into their early years setting.

- From Cuba: the idea that parents can be co-educators alongside early years professionals, and need support in this role.

To what extent are these ideas from other contexts present—in some form—in the Early Years Foundation Stage (EYFS), and in the practice you observe in early years settings? Which of these *could* be implemented—remember, they have all been highlighted as 'quality' practice! What might be the factors that would enable such initiatives? And what might be the barriers?

References

Blackwell, S., & Pound, L. (2011). Forest Schools in the early years. In L. Miller & L. Pound (Eds.), *Theories and approaches to learning in the early years.* London: Sage.

Brosterman, N. (1997). *Inventing kindergarten.* New York: Harry N Abrams.

Economist Intelligence Unit. (2012). *Starting well: Benchmarking early education across the world.* London: The Economist.

Gapminder. (2015). *Gapminder world: A fact-based worldview.* Retrieved 1 June, 2015, from http://www.gapminder.org/world/

Hewitt, V. (2001). Examining the Reggio Emilia approach to early childhood education. *Early Childhood Education Journal, 29*(2), 95–100.

Kahn, R. (2010). *Critical pedagogy, ecoliteracy, and planetary crisis.* New York: Peter Lang.

Learning and Teaching Scotland. (2006). *The Reggio Emilia approach to early childhood education* (2nd ed.). Glasgow: Learning and Teaching Scotland.

Malaguzzi, L. (1993). For an education based on relationship. *Young Children, 49*(1), 9–12.

New Zealand Ministry of Education. (1996). *Te Whāriki: Early childhood curriculum.* Retrieved 1 June, 2015, from http://www.educate.ece.govt.nz/learning/curriculumAndLearning/TeWhariki

Organization for Economic Co-operation and Development. (2001). *Starting strong: early. Childhood education and care.* Paris: OECD.

Organization for Economic Co-operation and Development. (2006). *Starting strong II: Early childhood education and care.* Retrieved June 1, 2015, from http://www.oecd.org/edu/preschoolandschool/37519079.pdf

Podmore, V., May, H., & Carr, M. (2001). The 'child's questions': Programme evaluation with Te Whrāiki using 'Teaching Stories'. *Early Childhood Folio, 5,* 6–9.

Taguma, M., Litjens, I., & Makowiecki, K. (2013). *Quality matters in early childhood education and care: Sweden.* Paris: Organization for Economic Co-operation and Development (OECD).

Tinajero, A. (2010). *Scaling up early child development in Cuba.* Washington, DC: Brookings Institute.

United Nations Children's Fund. (2000). Defining quality in education. *Proceedings from The International Working Group on Education, Florence, Italy.*

United Nations Children's Fund. (2010). *Child-friendly schools.* Retrieved June 1, 2015, from http://www.unicef.org/education/index_focus_schools.html

United Nations Children's Fund. (2011). *School readiness.* Retrieved June 1, 2015, from http://www.unicef.org/education/index_44888.html

United Nations Children's Fund. (2014). *A Summary of the rights under the Convention on the Rights of the Child.* London: United Nations Children's Fund (UNICEF).

United Nations Educational, Scientific and Cultural Organization. (2006). *Cuba: Early childhood care and education (ECCE) programmes.* Paris: UNESCO.

Uunited Nations General Assembly. (1989). *Convention on the Rights of the Child, 20 November 1989.* United Nations Treaty Series, Vol. 1577.

Watling, R., & Clarke, S. (1995). 'Our village': Freire, Freinet and practical media work in the early years. *Early Years: An International Journal of Research and Development, 15*(2), 6–12.

10 Quality in early years research

Patrick Carmichael

The relationship between educational research and practice is not an easy one. Over many years, there have frequently been concerns voiced about the 'quality' of educational research. But there are, as Boaz and Ashby (2003) explain, many things that *should* guarantee that research is of high quality: these include published standards, checklists, how-to guides and textbooks; and research is subject to peer review both at the proposal stage and when its results are published. 'With all this activity', asks Boaz and Ashby, 'why the debate about quality?' (2003, p. 3). Part of the issue, Boaz and Ashby suggest, is that while these 'best practices' may be applied to large-scale funded research in universities and government departments, they may not be accessible to researchers and evaluators working in local authority settings, or to teacher-researchers or students who are attempting to develop practice and provision in their own work settings.

A further criticism of educational research is that much of it—including that which satisfies the demands of research funders and publishers of academic journals—is not relevant to what teachers actually do and the day-to-day challenges they face. This has led to government funding for educational research being directed towards enquiries into finding 'what works' in educational settings. We have seen this reflected in projects like Effective Provision of Pre-School Education (EPPE) and other enquiries into what contributes quality, where researchers draw on evidence of different kinds and try and identify what are the key factors, prerequisites or practices that lead to desirable outcomes.

This dual concern with quality and relevance has led to researchers in education being encouraged to draw on the experience of medical sciences, using evidence gathered from experiments and randomized control trials to support 'evidence-informed practice' by 'research-informed teachers'. It is telling that the UK Government turned to Ben Goldacre, a doctor and medical researcher, and author of a column in *The Guardian* named 'Bad Science', to write a briefing paper 'Building evidence into education' (Goldacre, 2013). This advocates medical-style trials of educational initiatives and classroom practice, with the intention of making teaching a truly 'evidence-based profession'.

In 2015, the Education Endowment Foundation (EEF), which has been central in promoting this approach to the use of educational research in practice, published a review of research in early years education. This report attempted to quantify the cost, strength of evidence and impact of a range of strategies including 'early literacy', 'earlier starting age', 'parental engagement' and 'self-regulation strategies' (all seen as effective, although with different amounts of research evidence) and 'physical environment' (on which the evidence was not strong and the impact remained unproven) (Education Endowment Foundation, 2015). The impacts of these strategies are measured in 'average months progress', demonstrating the tendency to measure impact on a normative and linear developmental scale, as Perry Knight argues in Chapter 5.

Gert Biesta, a philosopher of education, has critiqued the assumptions behind these approaches, and argues that while focusing on evidence-based practice provides a simple way of thinking about what research might offer, it also limits the kinds of questions that researchers might ask, and the kinds of outcomes for which they might look (Biesta, 2007). There are other traditions of educational research that invite educational professionals to ask different kinds of questions, and use research approaches other than experiments and trials. Participatory action research, for example, involves researchers, practitioners and other participants identifying areas of interest or concern, gathering information and planning, intervening and then reflecting on outcomes together. Action researchers such as John Elliot suggest that rather than research being concerned to find 'what works' across *all* educational settings, the involvement of a range of interested parties in a 'deliberative' enquiry into specific settings, issues or practices is the key to educational improvement (Elliott, 2009).

Successful action research involves the commitment of time and energy by a range of stakeholders, and does not promise 'quick fixes' to educational challenges—although the changes it brings about have the potential to be effective and long-lasting, as they are embedded within the practice of the particular setting. For action research to be effective, educational leaders must create a culture in which experimentation and innovation 'from below' are supported and encouraged. It may be difficult for the individual teacher-researcher or student to initiate action research in an environment whose leaders are concerned about outcomes and so are 'risk-averse', and where the researchers have limited power to act.

Reflection point 10.1

- Think about the research that you have drawn on as your practice has developed. What kind of research was it: reports of large-scale experiments or surveys; accounts of interventions and action research; or case studies, narratives and observations by practitioners? You may need to revisit some of your reading, and if you only have a summary of research findings or outcomes, you may need to dig deeper to find out how those were reached.

- How did the research affect your understanding and practice? Given the criticisms mentioned above, what contributes to research being 'relevant'?

Framing research in early years

It is important to recognize the difference between 'research into quality' (which tries to understand quality practice and provision, and to identify the factors that might contribute to these) and 'quality research', which might be much broader in its scope and aims. In the remainder of this chapter we will consider a number of ways in which you might plan and put into practice a research project of your own. You might be required to do this as part of a dissertation project as part of an early years teacher course, or to provide evidence of the leadership of change in a portfolio, or as part of a day-to-day leadership role within an early years setting. And while you might do this with the intention of improving the provision of education and care, it may be that this comes about not because you identify a simple 'cause-and-effect' or 'what works' pattern, but rather through your gaining a better understanding of children's learning or new insights into the lives of their families or communities, through establishing new relationships, or by sharing knowledge more effectively.

The current enthusiasm for evidence-informed practice and demonstrating impact (in development months or in some other way) leads many teachers and student teachers to assume that they have to carry out measurements, surveys or intervention studies with 'pre-tests' and 'post-tests'. These do have their place, but more important than any particular research design is the notion of 'fitness for purpose'. In other words, once an area of interest or concern has been identified (often through discussion with others), research questions are developed and then (and only then) are appropriate means of exploring them identified. It may well be that an early years setting, having implemented a new programme of some kind, wants to evaluate it; in this case, gathering evidence of how (or if!) it has had an impact on children's engagement, participation or development will be entirely appropriate. But in many early years settings, what is most 'fit for purpose' for researching children's needs, experiences and holistic development may be different.

In their discussion of a research agenda for early years, Broadhead, Howard, and Wood (2010) propose how early years research should be framed and conducted. They highlight a number of key aspects informed by their positioning of play at the centre both of pedagogy and research, namely that:

- research should be underpinned by a commitment to understanding and extending children's rights: not just in the sense that their involvement in research should be governed by ethical practices, or that their privacy should be guaranteed, for example, but that efforts should be made to listen to their voices and that their concerns and choices should be respected as part of a 'deep pedagogical responsibility'. (Broadhead et al., 2010, p. 179)
- observation, including non-participant observation, focused interactions, direct teaching and sustained engagement alongside children, represents the best way of understanding the 'ideas, imaginings and intentions' of children. (Broadhead et al., 2010, p. 182)

- meaning emerges through collaboration and critical, 'team-based' reflection on how best to build these developing understandings into professional practice (Broadhead et al., 2010, p. 182); in other words, through the kinds of critical participatory action research advocated by, among others, Elliott (2009) and Kemmis, (2011).

A good example of such an enquiry is Elizabeth Coates's work on young children's drawing (Coates, 2002), in which the starting point is her observation that while drawing children often talk to themselves. In a later version of the paper in which she also provides a very useful commentary on the processes of researching and writing, Coates (2004) describes how she carefully carried out unobtrusive, exploratory research in which she began to uncover the richness and complexity of the story-telling and meaning-making in which the children were involved. Even this small study (Coates is clear about its limitations) has implications for practice, suggesting that rather than asking children to 'tell us about the picture' after the event, the early years teacher may learn more by working alongside the child as they draw, listening attentively, sharing in the story-telling and scaffolding learning through timely questions. This is another way in which research can be made 'fit for purpose', by aligning it with established pedagogical practice in naturalistic settings, rather than using intrusive methods or setting up artificial experiments.

The challenge that these approaches present is how best to communicate the outcomes or findings of research beyond the immediate setting and how to influence or inform other people's practice, or policy across a network of schools, Children's Centres, more widely (across a local authority, for example), or even nationally or globally. Altrichter, Posch, and Somekh (1993) suggest that sharing knowledge about educational research is essential for a number of reasons, some of which contribute indirectly or directly to the quality of practice. They identify the following benefits:

- It prevents teacher knowledge from being forgotten.
- It increases the quality of reflection on practice.
- It allows teachers to clarify their own position and bring influence to bear on educational policy by means of rational argument.
- It allows teachers to meet the requirements of professional accountability.
- It allows teachers to play a more active role in teacher professional development and initial teacher education.
- It reinforces teachers' professional self-confidence. (1993, pp. 173–176)

In later work, Altrichter (2005) discusses how this sharing of practical knowledge can be enabled in the kinds of 'communities of practice' described by Wenger (1998), and also describes how it may be most effective when teachers gradually share their work with what he describes as 'graded publics'—beginning with their closest colleagues in their own setting, then progressing to whole-setting or community engagement, before considering how to disseminate their findings, interpretations and recommendations more widely. This allows teachers to gradually build confidence in both the quality of their research approaches and findings, and in talking or writing about them for people beyond their immediate working environments.

One of the distinctive aspects of working and researching in early years settings is the involvement of stakeholders and professionals with different backgrounds, concerns and perspectives on children's learning, development and care (a theme we have discussed at various points elsewhere in this book). This can make research more interesting and challenging, and means that the teacher-researcher may have to engage with different notions of quality in relation to the research questions they might investigate, the evidence they might gather and the claims they might make as a result. It is not difficult to imagine a situation in which an observational, rights-based enquiry of the kind advocated by Broadhead et al. (2010) resonates with many teachers, but is seen as being unsatisfactory by others (managers, local authority leaders or policymakers) who would prefer unequivocal messages about what will 'work' to improve outcomes or increase the numbers of children who achieve a 'good level of development', for example.

The anthropologist Marilyn Strathern argues that engaging in this dialogue is an important aspect of interdisciplinary and inter-professional working. Rather than seeing it as a process by which a range of professionals work together on problems or challenges and where each makes a contribution to finding a solution, she suggests instead that working together allows participants to 'make visible the interests of those who are identifiably "other"' (Strathern, 2009, p. 203), supporting reflection on existing practice and informing the development of new notions of quality (Strathern, 2004). So the early years teacher may find that engaging in research not only contributes to their own practice, but also allows them to share their approaches and 'interests' with others, while at the same time developing a greater understanding of what is important from the perspectives of other stakeholders and professionals with whom they work. Sometimes, it is the discovery that people 'think differently' (about a particular child, a family, a location, or an aspect of learning or care) that represents the most important finding of a research project, and allows a rethinking of what quality provision and practice might involve.

Reflection point 10.2

- Where have you encountered findings from research? By hearing about it from the person who carried it out? By reading, in books, journals or online? Or is it reflected in particular practices or processes in which you are involved?

- If you were going to carry out a research project, who might you involve? Where and how might you disseminate your findings? Who are your potential 'participants' and your 'publics'?

Carrying out quality research in early years settings

In the last section of this final chapter in the book, we will explore some of the issues that you might need to consider if you were involved in some kind of research enquiry into practice and provision in early years. You might be undertaking a project as part of a course, or as an element in a portfolio of evidence, or as part of a school-based initiative or improvement plan. In the first case, you should see this chapter as accompanying whatever guidance you receive from tutors or mentors: the requirements of your particular course should take precedence over the general guidelines given here.

Any of the themes discussed in previous chapters could form the basis of a research project that represents 'quality research', both in the sense that it stands up to scrutiny from an academic perspective, and that it improves understanding or practice. You might, for example, explore the nature of professionalism or how professional identities are formed (Chapter 2); the role the environment plays in promoting learning or social development (Chapter 4); relationships, support and how people from different agencies work together (Chapters 5 and 9); the ways in which policies and curricula are constructed, enacted and 'mediated' through pedagogy (Chapters 7 and 8); or the particular practices that accompany working with babies (Chapter 3) or vulnerable children (Chapter 6).

Whether you are planning to carry out your research as part of a course requirement or not, you will need to engage with the potential participants and convince them first that you should be allowed to do it and second that they should take part. Your participants, remember, may include not only adults (colleagues, governors, managers, parents) but also children. In order to engage these groups, while at the same time maintaining the quality of your research, you will need to keep a number of issues in mind.

First, it is important that the research you undertake is 'research-worthy': in other words, that it is worth your time, and that of others being spent on it; that it is not trivial; and that it does not collect information that already exists. There are few things more irritating for busy research participants than being asked questions when the answers are already well documented, possibly by themselves. It is worth remembering that not all stakeholders may share your enthusiasm for your proposal or think it worthy of research—so you may need to build a case for 'why this project', 'why here' and 'why now'?

Second, any proposed project has to be 'researchable'. This involves formulating research questions and choosing the fit-for-purpose research approaches in such a way that you actually have some chance of answering them given the limitations of access, time and resources you probably face. Beginning researchers often propose projects that are much too broad in its scope, and the development of a research proposal may involve narrowing initial ideas down into answerable questions. So, for example, 'How do young children learn with digital technologies?' is too broad: this would require a whole research programme that might involve many researchers from different disciplines. On the other hand, questions of the form 'How the can the use of digital technologies help young children develop fine motor skills?' or 'How best can teachers integrate the use of new technologies into outdoor play?' are not only more focused, they also give some indication of what research approaches (observations, looking at children's productions, interviews, and so on) might be most appropriate. It is better to produce a small-scale piece of quality research with the potential to influence practice than something that is too broad and probably, as a result, too vague, to be useful.

Third, the project will need to be carried out in line with a consistent, appropriate ethical framework. Many educational researchers use the guidelines published by the British Educational Research Association (BERA) (2011) though the British Sociological Association (BSA) (2002) provides another appropriate framework and the National Society for the Prevention of Cruelty to Children (NSPCC) (2013) also is a good source of advice. More important than identifying a single framework to help you gain ethical 'approval' though, is that you behave ethically throughout your project. This involves behaving with the same concern for children's rights as any early years professional, and maintaining the 'ethic of care' that has been discussed elsewhere in the book. According to the United Nations Convention on the Rights of the Child (United Nations Children's Fund, 2014), all children (even very young ones) are the subjects of their own rights, and this includes the right not to take part in your research. Flewitt (2005) describes how children as young as 3 years old are capable of expressing their consent to take part in research enquiries, and they are certainly able to express the fact that they do *not* wish to participate! In fact, Flewitt suggests that young children's curiosity may mean that they ask more searching questions of you than their parents, carers or teachers.

Conducting research in an ethical way is not simply a matter of gaining approval and 'covering yourself' should anything go wrong: it involves obtaining informed consent, thinking about how to engage participants, and working through 'what-if' scenarios: 'What if the children are upset by my questions?' 'What if the *teachers* are upset by my questions?', 'What if my interviews uncover a safeguarding issue?', 'What if I cannot adequately guarantee anonymity to participants?'. Reflecting on these issues and potential dilemmas will contribute to the quality of your research, improving its potential impact on practice and, should you have the opportunity to publish your findings, their academic credibility as well.

A fourth, and related issue, concerns the way in which you, as a researcher, work in your research setting or settings. Just because you have a researchable, research-worthy project that has received ethical approval does not allow you to impose changes or make demands on teachers or children—your behaviour should be governed by the broader commitments to do no harm, maintain an ethic of care and respect the rights of research participants. What this means in practice is that it is essential that you consult with teachers, managers, parents and carers prior to making changes or experimenting, in order that what you are proposing is not at odds with the ethos of the setting and the values of those who work and learn there. So, for example, a setting with a highly inclusive ethos and the practices that accompany it will not be the place to start experimenting with 'ability grouping', nor will a setting in which the practice and environment is influenced by *Reggio Emilia* approaches (as described in Chapter 4) take kindly to you experimenting with highly teacher-directed activities in pursuit of a particular learning outcome.

Finally, your research needs to reflect your own beliefs and values, and should contribute to your developing a sense of 'self' both as a researcher and as an early years professional. The kind of research that we have discussed in this book, with its emphasis on observation, interpretation, reflection and participation, does not demand that you stand apart from the research or its participants as a disinterested data collector. Norman Denzin argues that this kind of research 'begins and ends with the biography and self of the researcher' (Denzin, 2002, p. 12). In other words, researchers need to be aware of what they bring to an enquiry (interests, assumptions, experience, insights) and what they might take away from it. According to this perspective, research is not something separate from your work as a teacher, but rather an episode or set of activities that is intrinsic to it and will contribute to your continuing professional development. It does demand, however, that you reflect on your own 'positioning' and the ways in which this has not only biased, but has also inspired, influenced and shaped your research study (Mantzoukas, 2005).

An example: talk in the home corner

When you are planning a project, it is often worth imagining that you are making a kind of 'sales pitch' in which you have to explain who you are, what you are planning to do and why, to each of the potential stakeholders and participants. This is worth doing not only so that you are prepared for their questions, but also to strengthen your own understanding and as a way of uncovering any assumptions you may be making as you plan your research. The vignette below is a good example of a small research project that needed some 'thinking through' in this way:

> **Vignette**
>
> Andrea was carrying out a project as part of her initial teacher training. She was interested in how children who seemed to have few conversations with adults talked animatedly while playing in the 'home corner' or other role-play areas of the early years base in her placement school. She prepared a project plan in which she would interview teachers about this, would look at children's 'learning journey' records for evidence, and then would observe children in a number of activities in the early years base. She asked the head teacher for permission to carry out the project and they were very interested and supportive, not least because some of the

children were failing to achieve 'expected' levels of progress in language, and the project might help her and her staff to understand better how to support them.

Once Andrea had, with the help of staff, identified a number of children on whom she was going to focus her observations, she observed the class as a whole and made some notes about their patterns of play and interaction. Later, she settled herself into a space close to the 'home corner' with a discreet audio-recorder and her notebook ready. A group of children, including (she was pleased to see) one of those in whom she was most interested, came into the home corner and, seeing her there, stopped and looked at her quizzically. 'What are you doing?' one asked. 'Oh, don't worry about me', Andrea replied, and made some suggestions about what they might do with the objects set out around the home corner. The children played for a short while, all the time watching Andrea, but there was little conversation or apparent purpose to their activities. After a few minutes the doors to the outside area were opened and the children took this as an opportunity to leave and were soon engaged in another activity outdoors. Andrea was disappointed and realized that she might need to approach this aspect of her project in a different way.

Andrea's story (not her real name) is based on a real student project. Clearly, Andrea had made her 'pitch' in such a way that the head teacher and class teachers were happy for her to proceed, and she had identified an authentic 'research-worthy' focus that addressed a real concern; but when it came to engaging the young participants in her project, she obviously had some work to do to make her methods fit for purpose and the whole question 'researchable'.

Reflection point 10.3

- How might Andrea have introduced herself and her project to the children?
- If you were in her position how would you have entered the play area?
- How would you have explained who you were and why you wanted to spend time with the children?

In Andrea's case, the key lay in conveying to the children her interest in their play and interactions in such a way that they were happy for her to be present. She also had to be sure that her presence did not either constrain their activities (including the talk in which she was interested, of course) while at the same time not coercing them into activities that were artificial or 'performed' simply so that she could collect data. After some thought, Andrea returned to the classroom and the home corner and this time positioned herself more as a 'helper' for the children, inviting them to suggest activities and playing alongside them. When a child (who recognized that she was not one of the usual group of adults they encountered in the classroom) asked her who she was and why she was there, she responded that she was 'a new teacher, and I wanted to find out about what you like doing, and how you play together'. To her surprise (and delight) the children not only accepted this explanation, but also began to explain to her what they were doing, what they did in other areas of the setting, and took her with them to other areas where they played together to show her what they were doing.

In the course of this 'co-research' *with* the children (rather than 'on' or about' them), Andrea discovered the areas of the setting in which her quiet children felt safe to talk, as well as the people they talked to, and the things that they talked about—providing a far deeper understanding than her initial observational approach would have ever done, and one that could directly inform her practice. The insights she gained from the project gave her a 'child's eye' view of the setting, made her think about the organization of spaces within early years settings in general, and (perhaps most critically) made her reassess how she might engage with young children, and assess and support their learning and development.

Each of the aspects we have discussed here (research-worthiness, researchability, ethical practice, respect for the ethos of the research setting and reflection on the role of research in your professional identity) has a contribution to make to quality, not only of the research project itself, but also of early years practice in general. Andrea's story is more about her development as a professional with a commitment to children's learning than about the completion of a successful research project, and is just as much about good early years practice as it is about educational research methods.

A final note

Throughout this book we have considered a range of key elements of early years practice that influence quality early years provision. Using your own initial ideas of key ingredients that determine 'quality' as a backdrop, subsequent chapters have helped you to enact these to ensure a quality early years experience for young children. We have also considered how you can maintain quality in your practice with very young or vulnerable children, even if the curriculum you are required to adhere to does not always sit neatly with your own ideas. The dissonance that this might create was further explored in relation to how this informs your professional identity, both as an individual and as a collective community of professionals.

And now, finally, we have looked at how professional enquiry, like practice, needs to respond to these same complexities. Well-designed, ethically sound research or enquiry has the potential not only to contribute to your own professional abilities and practices, such as the ability to evaluate, develop and lead quality practice, but also in moving closer to determining and understanding just what it is that make quality early years practice. The core ideas presented within this book serve as a reminder that notions of quality might never be 'static' and thus it is a notion that you should continually reflect upon, challenge and consider if you are to ensure that young children—both now and in the future—have the best quality provision and, therefore, the best possible life chances.

References

Altrichter, H. (2005). The role of the professional community in action research. *Educational Action Research, 13*(1), 11–23.

Altrichter, H., Posch, P., & Somekh, B. (1993). *Teachers investigate their work: An introduction to the methods of action research.* London: Routledge.

British Educational Research Association. (2011). *Ethical guidelines for educational research.* London: BERA.

Biesta, G. (2007). Why 'what works' won't work: Evidence-based practice and the democratic deficit in educational research. *Educational Theory, 57,* 1–22.

Boaz, A., & Ashby, D. (2003). *Fit for purpose? Assessing research quality for evidence based policy and practice (ESRC UK Centre for Evidence Based Policy and Practice: Working Paper 11).* Swindon: Economic and Social Reseach Council (ESRC).

British Sociological Association. (2002). *Statement of ethical practice.* London: BSA.

Broadhead, P., Howard, J., & Wood, E. (2010). Understanding playful learning and playful pedagogies: Towards a new research agenda. In P. Broadhead, J. Howard, & E. Wood (Eds.), *Play and learning in the early years: From research to practice* (pp. 177–186). London: Sage.

Coates, E. (2002). 'I forgot the sky!' Children's stories contained within their drawings. *International Journal of Early Years Education, 10*(1), 21–35.

Coates, E. (2004). 'I forgot the sky!' Children's stories contained within their drawings. In V. Lewis, M. Kellett, M. Robinson, S. Fraser, & S. Ding (Eds.), *The reality of research with children and young people* (pp. 5–26). London: Sage.

Denzin, N. (2002). *Interpretive interactionism* (2nd ed.). London: Sage.

Education Endowment Foundation. (2015). *Early years toolkit.* Retrieved from https://educationendowmentfoundation.org.uk/toolkit/early-years/

Elliott, J. (2009). Research-based teaching. In S. Gewirtz, P. Mahony, I. Hextall, & A. Cribb (Eds.), *Changing teacher professionalism: International trends, challenges and ways forward* (pp. 170–183). London: Routledge.

Flewitt, R. (2005). Conducting research with young children: Some ethical considerations. *Early child development and care, 175*(6), 553–565.

Goldacre, B. (2013). *Building evidence into education*. London: Department for Education (DfE).

Kemmis, S. (2011). A self-reflective practitioner and a new definition of critical participatory action research. In N. Mockler & J. Sachs (Eds.), *Rethinking educational practice through reflexive inquiry* (pp. 11–29). Dordrecht: Springer.

Mantzoukas, G. (2005). The inclusion of bias in reflective and reflexive research: A necessary prerequisite for securing validity. *Journal of Research in Nursing, 10*(3), 279–295.

National Society for the Prevention of Cruelty to Children (2013). *Conducting safe and ethical research with children: An NSPCC factsheet*. London: NSPCC.

Strathern, M. (2004). *Commons and borderlands*. Wantage: Sean Kingston Books.

Strathern, M. (2009). A community of critics: Thoughts on new knowledge. *Journal of the Royal Anthropological Institute, 12*(1), 191–209.

United Nations Children's Fund. (2014). *A summary of the rights under the convention on the Rights of the Child*. London: UNICEF.

Wenger, E. (1998). *Communities of practice: Learning, meaning and identity*. Cambridge: Cambridge University Press.

Index

activities, child
    comparison of indoor and
        outdoor, 44
    see also factors
        effecting quality
        e.g. environments,
        learning
    see also purposes of e.g.
        creativity, child
Adams, G., 17
Allen, G., 123
Altrichter, H., 155
Ana (vignette)
    policies about safe touch
        in settings, 95
Andrea (vignette)
    conducting quality
        research in settings,
        159–60
Anjum (vignette)
    early years
        professionalism, 124
Ann (vignette)
    emergent-progressive
        curriculum in action,
        82–3
    power of supervision as
        support for staff, 67
    transitions into early
        years setting, 20
Ansari, W., 44
Arnett Caregiver Interaction
    Scale (CIS), 4
Ashby, D., 152
Ashkanasy, N.M., 130
assessment, early years
    impact on construction
        of quality environ-
        ments, 46
Atkinson, P., 131
attachment
    importance for successful
        early childhood,
        17–19

Aubrey, C., 83
austerity, economic
    impact on practitioner
        professionalism,
        119–26

babies
    characteristics of
        high-quality care and
        education, 16–17
    importance of attachment
        for successful early
        years, 17–19
    importance and
        characteristics of
        transition into early
        childcare, 19–21
    importance of caring in
        childcare setting,
        22–3
    need for knowledge and
        skills for care of,
        23–4
    need for practitioners
        to both care and
        educate, 24–6
    need for quality support
        for practitioners
        caring for, 26–8
Baby P. case (2007), 134
Banks, S., 120–21
benchmarks, quality
    publications providing,
        11–13
Bereiter, C., 127, 128
Berthelsten, D., 53
Biesta, G., 153
Birth to Three Matters
    (DfES, 2002), 1, 25, 51
boards, advisory
    need for quality relation-
        ships with practition-
        ers, 58–9
Boaz, A., 152

Bowlby, J., 19, 21
Brendon, M., 103
British Educational
    Research Association
    (BERA), 158
British Sociological
    Association (BSA), 158
Britt, D., 20
Broadhead, P., 154, 156
Bronfenbrenner, U., 78, 134
Brown, R., 113
Brownlee, J., 52
Bruce, T., 79
Bruner, J., 76
Building Evidence into
    Education
    (Goldacre), 152

Cabral, C., 103
care and caring, early years
    see education, early
        years
Carlen, P., 103
Carr, M., 37–8, 39, 41, 42,
    79, 146
Carter, M., 45
Chawla-Duggan, R., 33
Child Protection (Dept. for
    Health, 1995), 106
Child Protection Committee
    (Scotland), 111
childcare, early years see
    education, early years
Childcare Act (2006), 123
children, very young
    characteristics of
        high-quality care and
        education, 16–17
    comparison of indoor and
        outdoor activities
        of, 44
    importance of attachment
        for successful early
        years, 17–19

importance of caring in childcare setting, 22–3

importance of time to enable creativity of, 43

importance of transition into early childcare, 19–21

need for knowledge and skills for care of, 23–4

need for practitioners to both care and educate, 24–6

need for quality relationships with other children, 51–3

need for quality relationships with practitioners, 51

need for quality support for practitioners caring for, 26–8

see also factors affecting development e.g. environments, learning

children, vulnerable definition, characteristics and context, 100–101

drivers and guidance on risk and vulnerability, 101–4

knowledge of effective early help, 109–12

policy and legislative framework, 104–9

see also Special Educational Needs or Disabilities

see also type e.g. looked after children

Children Act (1989), 104–5, 105–6, 113

Children Act (2004), 105

Children's Centres, 2, 8, 21, 60, 89, 109, 148, 155

Children's' Workforce Development Council, 7–8

Clarke, A., 35

Claxton, G., 36, 37–8, 39, 41, 42

Coates, E., 155

Coffey, A., 131

cognition Piaget's stages of, 76–8

Colley, H., 125

Common Assessment Framework (CAF), 109–10

continuing professional development (CPD) Children's centres as source of, 60, 62

role and importance in sustaining quality practice, 63–4

see also networks, early years; qualifications; supervision

Convention on the Rights of the Child (UN, 1989), 10–11, 34, 140–42, 158

Cooper, M., 79–80

Cousins, S., 21

creativity, child importance of provision of time to enable, 43

see also factors influencing e.g. curriculum, early years, environments, learning; skills and knowledge

Crowley, K., 46

Cuba community education in as example of early years quality, 147–

curriculum, early years historical pathway of development, 74–5

importance within early years context, 73–4

models and perspectives, 78–9

models developing holistic and individualised curriculum, 81–5

nature of, 76–8

quality curricula within EYFS framework, 79–81

see also factors affecting e.g. policies, governmental

Curtis, D., 45

Dahl, S., 83

Dahlberg, G., 55

Dau, E., 84

De Gaetano, Y., 32

Dearnley, K., 51

Debbie (vignette) early years professionalism, 124

Denzin, N., 159

development, cognitive Piaget's stages of, 76–8

development and experiences, child importance of environment for enabling social and emotional, 33–4, 41–2

Development Matters (Early Education, 2012), 45, 89–90

Dewey, J., 56

Donnellan, H., 132

Dowling, M., 74

Down, S., 128–9

Dunn, J., 52

Dweck, C., 36, 42

Dyson, C., 103

Early Childhood Education and Care (ECEC, Sweden), 144–6

Early Childhood Environment Rating Scale (ECERS), 4, 30

early years care and education see education, early years

Early Years Foundation Stage (EYFS) framework, 1–2, 23, 25, 31, 35, 43, 46, 55, 76, 77, 78, 79–81, 82, 83, 84, 85–6, 90, 91–4, 118–19, 122, 138

Early Years Foundation Stage Profile (EYFSP), 64

Early Years Inspection Handbook (Ofsted, 2015), 25

Early Years Outcomes (DfE, 2013), 90

Early Years Professional Status (EYPS), 122

Early Years Teacher Status (EYTS), 61, 90

Early Years Transitions and Special Educational Needs (EYTSEN) project, 7

Edgington, M., 56

'Educate Your Child' programme (Cuba), 148–9

education, early years
characteristics of high quality, 16–17
conducting quality research on, 157–9
criticisms of research of, 152–3
definitions and importance in early years childcare, 22–3
framing of research on, 154–6
global perspectives on quality, 10–11
importance and characteristics of transitions into early childcare, 19–21
importance of attachment for successful, 17–19
importance of love in childcare settings, 21, 23
importance of practitioner 'caring,' 22–3
international exemplification of quality of, 143–50
international measurements of quality, 140–43
need for knowledge and skills for care of babies, 23–4
need for practitioners to both educate and, 24–6

need for quality support for practitioners, 26–8
projects and studies defining and developing quality, 5–8
rating scales measuring quality, 4–5
stakeholder perceptions of quality, 8–10
see also research, early years
see also elements e.g. children, vulnerable; curriculum, early years; environments, learning
see also factors ensuring e.g. continuing professional development; leadership; networks, early years; policies, governmental; qualifications; relationships, quality; supervision
see also features required e.g. attachment; love
see also players e.g. babies; children, very young; practitioners, early years

Education Endowment Foundation (EEF), 152–3

Effective Provision of Pre-School Education (EPPE) project, 6, 61, 75, 152

Elfer, P., 21, 23, 26, 27, 51, 52, 128

Elliott, J., 153, 155

emergent curriculum model, 82

Emerson, R.W., 139

Emma (vignette)
emergent play-based curriculum in action, 84

emotions, child
learning environment for developing and enhancing, 33–4, 41–2

emotions, practitioner
impact on professionalism of, 129–32

environments, learning
centrality of talk, 34–5
challenges facing development of quality, 45–6
characteristics of enabling child resilience and growth, 36–7
creating a potential, 39–41
elements and influences required to shape quality, 37–9
impact of assessment on construction of quality, 46
importance of play, 35
need for flexibility of, 42
need for good quality for successful learning, 31–3
need for time for child exploration and creativity, 43
organisation of to encourage social experiences, 41–2
to enhance social and emotional development, 33–4
see also types of environment e.g. outdoors

e-safety policies, 96–7

'ethic of care' (Noddings), 22

Every Child a Talker (ECaT) programme, 67

Every Child Matters (HM Treasury, 2003), 105, 123

evolving curriculum model, 83–4

experiences and development, child
importance of environment for enabling social and emotional, 33–4, 41–2

'expert,' professional practitioners as, 127–9

exploration, child
importance of provision
of time to enable, 43

Family Childhood Rating
Scale (FCRS), 5
Featherstone, B., 103
Filmer-Sankey, C., 110
Flewitt, R., 158
flexibility
importance of in
developing learning
environments, 42
Flori (vignette)
policies about safe touch
in settings, 95
Forest schools, 82, 85, 139
Fraenkel, P., 17
Francis, B., 131
Freire, P., 139
Froebel, F., 138

Gapminder Project, 142
Gardner, D., 21
Gasper, M., 133, 134
Gerhardt, S., 21, 52
Gibbs, G., 65
Gillentine, J., 95
Gleeson, D., 103
Goldacre, B., 152
Goldschmied, E., 23, 51
Goldstein, L., 22
Gooouch, K., 27
Gorin, S., 103
governors
need for quality
relationships with
practitioners, 58–9
growth and resilience, child
learning environments
enabling, 36–7
Guile, D., 61
Gupta, A., 103

Hammersley, M., 131
Härtel, C.E.J., 130
Hedges, H., 79–80
help and intervention
knowledge of effective
early, 109–12
vignettes of vulnerable
child, 107–8
Hendrick, H., 103

Hewitt, V., 144
'home corner,' 40, 159–61
Hooper, C.A., 103
Hoschschild, A.R., 129
Howard, J., 46, 154

Infant and Toddler
Environment Rating
Scale (ITERS), 4
infants see babies
internationalism
as example of early years
education quality,
143–50
impact on early
years learning
measurement, 140–43
intervention and help
knowledge of effective
early, 109–12
vignettes of vulnerable
child, 107–8

Jack (vignette)
emergent play-based cur-
riculum in action, 84
Jack, G., 132
Jackson, S., 51
Jarman, E., 34
Johns, C., 65
Joshua (vignette)
help and intervention with
vulnerable children,
107

Kahn, R., 139
Kemmis, S., 155
key person
need for quality relationship with child, 51
see also practitioners,
early years
see also ways of enhanc-
ing e.g. continuing
professional devel-
opment; networks,
early years; qualifi-
cations, supervision
knowledge and skills
need for in care of babies
and very young, 23–4
Kolb, D., 65
Kozulin, A., 73–4

Laming Report (2003), 134
Laura (vignette)
early years
professionalism, 124
Lave, J., 127, 128, 129
leadership
need for pedagogical
leadership to sustain
quality, 61
role and importance of
qualifications in
sustaining quality,
61–3
see also factors support-
ing e.g. continuing
professional devel-
opment; networks,
early years; qualifi-
cations; supervision
learning
strands of (EYFS), 80
see also education, early
years
Lee, W., 79
legislation
on vulnerable children,
104–9
Litjens, L., 145
local authorities
need for quality
relationships with
practitioners, 59–60
Local Safeguarding
Children's Board, 111
Lofland, J., 131
looked after children
characteristics and
context, 113–14
Lowland, L.H., 131
Lucas, N., 61

McCreery, E., 75
McInnes, K., 46
Macmillan, M., 139
Makowiecki, K., 145
Malaguzzi, L., 54–5
Manning-Morton, J., 21, 24,
26, 52, 63
Martin, A., 130
Maskell-Graham, D., 113
Mathers, S., 9, 92–3
Maude, P., 43–4
May, H., 147

measurement and monitoring
international quality initiatives, 140–43
policies on quality monitoring, 97–8
see also tools, measurement
Melluish, E., 61–2
Merrill, S., 20
Michelle (vignette)
need for quality sibling relationships, 53
Miles, G., 46
Miller, L., 73, 75, 81, 82
Mirchandani, K., 130
models and perspectives
early year curriculum, 78–9
play-based curriculum, 84–5
progressive curriculum, 82–3
see also typologies
Montessori, M., 138–9
More Great Childcare (DfE, 2013), 11–12, 123
Morris, K., 103
Moss, P., 35, 55, 101
Moyles, J., 126
multi-agency working
impact on practitioner professionalism, 132–4
Munro, E., 111
Munro Report (2011), 121
Murray, L., 17, 19

National Children's Bureau (NCB), 68
National Curriculum (1988), 74
National Day Nurseries Association (NDNA), 68
National Quality Improvement Network (NQIN), 2–3
National Society for the Prevention of Cruelty to Children (NSPCC), 158
networks, early years
importance in sustaining quality practice, 68–9

Noddings, N., 22
Nutbrown Report (2012), 11–12, 58, 91–2, 93, 123

Oberheumer, P., 119
Observation Record of the Caregiving Environment (ORCE), 4
Ofsted, 45, 55–6, 59, 65, 97
Organization for Economic Cooperation and Development (OECD), 32, 35, 142, 145, 146
Osgood, J., 22–3, 26, 27, 95
outdoors
importance as quality learning environment, 43–5
see also Forest schools
Owen, P., 95

Page, J., 21, 26, 27
parents
need for quality relationships with practitioners, 53–5
Pence, A., 55
peripatetics
need for quality relationships with practitioners, 59–60
Pestalozzi, J.H., 138
Petrie, P., 101
Phillips, D., 17
Piaget, J., 18, 76–8
play
importance as element of learning environments, 34–5
play-based curriculum model, 84–5
Podmore, V., 147
policies, governmental
in settings promoting quality provision, 95–7
measuring and monitoring quality, 97–8
on vulnerable children, 104–9
quality in context of, 89–90

quality in government reviews, 91–4
Posch, P., 155
Powell , S., 27
practice, early years *see* education, early years
practitioners, early years
changing professional identity of, 118–19
definitions and interpretations of professionalism, 126–7
impact of austerity on professionalism and work of, 119–26
impact of emotion on professionalism of, 129–32
impact of multi-agency working on professionalism, 132–4
need for quality relationships, 51, 53–60
need for quality support for, 26–8
notion of as professional 'expert,' 127–9
publication benchmarks for, 11–13
see also education, early years
see also factors supporting e.g. continuing professional development; networks, early years; qualifications; policies, governmental; supervision
see also qualities required e.g. education, early years; love
see also targets of e.g. babies; children, very young; children, vulnerable
see also tools aiding e.g. curriculum, early years; Early Years Foundation Stage; environments, learning; National

Quality Improvement
Network; research,
early years
professionalism, practitioner
changing face of, 118–19
definitions and
interpretations,
126–7
impact of austerity,
119–26
impact of multi-agency
working, 132–4
impact of practitioner
emotions on, 129–32
notion of professional
'expert,' 127–9
progressive curriculum
model, 82–3

qualifications
role in sustaining leadership quality, 61–3
quality (concept)
in context of government
policies, 89–90
in government reviews,
91–4
quality, early years
education
EYFS and NQIN on, 1–3
global perspectives, 10–11
international exemplification of, 143–50
international measure-
ments of , 140–43
projects and studies
defining and
developing, 5–8
rating scales measuring,
4–5
stakeholder perceptions
of, 8–10
see also practitioners,
early years
see also elements e.g. curriculum, early years
see also factors affecting
e.g. environments,
learning; policies,
governmental
see also factors ensuring
e.g. intervention and
help; safety, child

see also features required
e.g. attachment; edu-
cation, early years;
love
rating scales, environment,
4–5
readiness, school, 2
Reggio Emilia, 78, 79,
143–4, 159
relationships, quality
definition and
characteristics, 50–51
need for quality child-
child, 51–3
need for quality
practitioner-child, 51
need for quality
practitioner-leader/
manager, 57–9
need for quality
practitioner-parent,
53–5
need for quality
practitioner-
practitioner, 55–7
need for quality
practitioner-wider
support staff, 59–60
see also factors ensuring
e.g. continuing
professional
development; leader-
ship; networks, early
years; qualifications;
supervision
research, early years
conducting of within
settings, 157–9
criticisms of, 152–3
defining and developing
quality, 5–8
framing of within settings,
154–6
Researching Effective
Pedagogy in the Early
Years (REPEY) project,
6–7, 63
resilience and growth, child
learning environments
enabling, 36–7
rights, of child
UN Convention on, 10–11,
34, 140–42, 158

Rinaldi, C., 144
risk, child
guidance on vulnerab:
and, 101–4
Roberts, R., 21
Rodd, J., 58
Rogoff, B., 32, 52
Role of the Named Person
(Scottish Government
2015), 111
Rowbotham, S., 108
'Russian doll'
(Bronfenbrenner), 78
safety, child
e-policies concerning,
96–7
policies about safe
touch, 95
see also children, vulnerable; intervention and
help; looked after
children; measure-
ment and monitoring;
quality, early years
education
Sammons, P., 61–2, 75
scales, environment rating,
4–5
Scardamalia, M., 127, 128
School Age Care
Environment Rating
Scale (SACERS), 5
'school readiness' (EYFS), 2
Selleck, D.Y., 23, 51
Senge, P., 56
Sharp, C., 110
siblings
need for quality relationships, 52–3
Sigmund, E., 44
Sigmundova, D., 44
Simon (vignette)
early years professional-
ism, 124
Siraj-Blatchford, I., 3–4,
61, 62
skills and knowledge
need for in care of babies
and very young, 23–4
social experiences, child
learning environments
developing and
enhancing, 33–4, 41–2